HEROES AND MARVELS
OF THE
MIDDLE AGES

HEROES
AND MARVELS
OF THE
MIDDLE AGES

JACQUES LE GOFF

Translated by
TERESA LAVENDER FAGAN

REAKTION BOOKS LTD

For Hanka (1934–2004)

Published by Reaktion Books Ltd
Unit 32, Waterside
44–48 Wharf Road
London N1 7UX, UK
www.reaktionbooks.co.uk

First published in English 2020
English-language translation copyright © Reaktion Books 2020

Originally published in French as *Héros et merveilles du Moyen Âge*,
© Éditions du Seuil, 2005 and 2008

Translated from the French by Teresa Lavender Fagan

This translation does not include the chapter 'La Mesnie Hellequin'
of the original French edition

Printed and bound in India by Replika Press Pvt. Ltd

A catalogue record for this book is available from the British Library

ISBN 978 1 78914 212 9

CONTENTS

PREFACE

The aim of this book is to reveal the importance of the imaginary in history, and then to show that the men and women of the Middle Ages created heroes and marvels that were destined to inspire dreams in the *longue durée*, many of them sublimated in social and material realities of the time: cathedrals, knights, love (Tristan and Iseult), games and performance (jongleurs, troubadours and trouvères), exceptional women existing between God and Satan (Melusina, Pope Joan, Iseult, Valkyrie). I mainly wanted to follow the avatars of the medieval imaginary in the *longue durée*, with its eclipses and awakenings. Those awakenings usually occurred with Romanticism, and even more so with new means of artistic expression: film and comics.

In the end, I hope to reveal how truly modern the Middle Ages really were.

INTRODUCTION

In this book I hope to introduce to the reader a new and developing field of history, the history of the imaginary, defined here by Évelyne Patlagean:

> The field of the imaginary is made up of all the representations that go beyond the limits posed by findings of experience and deductive sequences that this allows. That is to say, that each culture, every society, or every level of a complex society has its imaginary. In other words, the boundary between the real and the imaginary is proven to be variable, even though the territory it crosses always and everywhere remains the same, since it is none other than the entire realm of human experience, from the most collectively social to the most intimately personal.[1]

In my book *L'Imaginaire médiéval* I have also attempted to define the field, first by distinguishing it from related concepts, foremost that of representation.[2] Patlagean is right when she says that the imaginary brings together a set of representations, but this very general term encompasses any mental translation of a perceived external reality: 'The imaginary is part of the field of representation, but it occupies the part of the non-reproducing translation, not simply transposed into images of the mind, but creative, poetic in the etymological sense.' The imaginary goes beyond the territory of representation and is driven beyond it by fantasy in the strongest sense of the word. The imaginary builds and feeds legends and myths. It can be defined as a society's system of dreams, a civilization transforming the real into impassioned views of the mind. The imaginary must then be distinguished from the symbolic. The medieval West thought through the mode of a symbolic system, starting with the constant referral of the New Testament to the Old, of which it was the symbolic translation. To take the example of one of the marvels in this book as described by Victor Hugo, the poet says of Notre-Dame de Paris as seen by Quasimodo: 'The cathedral was not just society to him, but the entire universe, all of nature.' He is creating a symbolic cathedral, but also an imaginary cathedral because 'the entire church was preaching something fantastic, supernatural, horrible; eyes and mouths were opened here and there.'

We need also to distinguish between the imaginary and the ideological. The ideological is invested with a conception of the world that tends to impose on representation a meaning that perverts both the material 'real' and that other real, the 'imaginary'. Medieval thought and medieval speech were structured by this ideological, which put the imaginary at its service in order to be more persuasive: thus the theme of two broadswords symbolizing spiritual and temporal power was applied to ecclesiastical ideology by subordinating the temporal sword to the spiritual sword beside it, even though the sword is one of the elements of this medieval imaginary strongly infused with warrior passion. The term 'imaginary' may refer to the imagination, but the history of the imaginary is not a history of the imagination in the traditional sense. It is a history of the creation of images and how a society uses them to make it act and think, because they come out of the mentality, the sensibility and the culture that infuse and animate them.

This history has been made possible by the new use that historians have made of images over the last few decades.[3] Jean-Claude Schmitt, one of those who have dedicated themselves to this new way of viewing images, stresses that for the historian the new meaning of the image goes very well with the meanings of the term *imago* in the Middle Ages:

> This notion is indeed at the centre of the medieval concept of the world and man. It refers not only to figurative objects, but also to the 'images' of language, it also refers to the 'mental' images of meditation and memory, dreams and visions . . . The notion of image ultimately involves all of Christian anthropology since it is man that the Bible from its first words describes as an 'image': Yahweh says he has shaped man '*ad imaginem* and *similitudinem nostram*' (Genesis 1:26).[4]

The present book is therefore a collection of articulated texts and images and has been made possible by the scholarship and research of Frédéric Mazuy, the remarkable iconographer. It does not seek to present a global view of the medieval imaginary, only its main characteristics through certain well-known components of the collection. As the title indicates, it looks at heroes and marvels. The term 'hero', which in ancient times referred to a figure who was outstanding on account of his courage and victories, while not belonging to the higher realms of gods and demi-gods, disappeared from Western culture and language with the Middle Ages and Christianity. The men who were then considered heroes, without the word itself being spoken, were a new type of man, the saint, and a type of administrator promoted in the foreground, the king. I have devoted a book to these two categories of medieval 'heroes'.[5] The heroes we will look at here are high-ranking or ambitious figures who were defined other than as saints and kings. The Old French term that, in medieval terminology, is closest to what I want to describe here is *preux*, which at the end of the twelfth century went from adjective to substantive. The term from which the word 'prowess' emerges was related in the twelfth century to warrior values and courage, and most often describes a bold fellow, a good knight. In the thirteenth century it was mainly associated with courtly attributes of kindness, goodness and honesty. In the heroes presented here we will find such connections to warrior courage and courtliness. Some of these figures are historical, but they quickly became legendary, such as Charlemagne and El Cid. Others are semi-legendary, having evolved from obscure and sometimes uncertain origins to the status of hero, for example, the Briton King Arthur, encountered in a chronicle from the very early Middle Ages, or Count Roland, the real but very obscure nephew of Charlemagne.

Finally, others are purely legendary, such as the female pope, Pope Joan, and Robin Hood, a brigand knight, protector of the weak, associated with the world of the forest, who appeared in fourteenth-century chronicles with no convincing historical connection. Other indisputable examples are the fairy Melusina and the wizard Merlin. The first group shows that between history and legend, between reality and the imagination, the medieval imaginary constructed a mixed, blended world that was the stuff of reality arising from the unreality of beings that seduced the imaginations of men and women in the Middle Ages. The reader will note that I have not included any figure who did not attain legendary status in the Middle Ages or later. Joan of Arc, for example, did not strike the medieval imagination, and even after she became an almost legendary figure she was not really detached from history; or if she was, it was by becoming for some a true saint, and for others the bearer of a nationalist ideology. The reader will also see that the list of heroes presented here is essentially male. It corresponds well to the period, to the civilization that Georges Duby has called the 'Male Middle Ages'.[6] Yet the promotion of women, including those introduced through legend and myth, was not unheard-of in the Middle Ages – far from it – and I have included four women who were very different from each other. One of them, a character in a romance, is at the heart of the theme of courtly love. She is Iseult, whom I did not want to separate from Tristan, as their legend ruthlessly wanted to do – fortunately without success – and who exemplifies the presence of famous couples in the medieval social reality and imaginary: Abelard and Heloise, St Francis and St Clare of Assisi, Tristan and Iseult. Another woman is the product of the fantasies of clerics. She illustrates the fear that those harsh and clumsy leaders had of women, of the new Eve, of her charms and her spells. What a scandal, what a disaster, if a woman through treachery might intrude into the body and functions of a man, who alone was allowed to fill the position of pope. Out of that fear, that fantasy, the legendary Pope Joan was born.

The other two women in this book are supernatural. They are fairies, and they illustrate the presence within medieval Christianity of figures and themes bequeathed by pagan beliefs that had been fought over and more or less erased, or simply Christianized on the surface. From the pagan Germanic world there is Valkyrie, the virgin warrior who guards the doors to Valhalla, the Teutonic paradise. The other, Melusina, comes from the Celtic infernal world. I would like to point out here the importance to the medieval imaginary of what is somewhat loosely called 'popular culture'. Since this book does not focus on 'marvellous' objects, although we will find them alongside our heroes, there are no chapters devoted to these objects that were so important in the medieval imaginary: swords (such as Charlemagne's Joyeuse, Roland's Durandal and Arthur's Excalibur); horns, the most famous of which is that of Roland; potions, which play such a large role in the story of Tristan and Iseult; and, finally, the mysterious and mystical object that is found at the highest level of the chivalrous ideal, the Holy Grail.

Apart from individual figures, we will see collective figures who haunted the medieval imaginary. As mentioned regarding the *preux*, they were associated with warrior courage, or chivalry, or both. These were the knights, at the heart of the chivalrous imaginary, and the troubadours, at the centre of the courtly imaginary. I have included among them the jongleur, that great entertainer of medieval seigniorial society, the playful creator of games and laughter.

Just as kings and saints have been presented elsewhere, likewise other higher beings will not be encountered here. The countless beings who populated the sky and the underworld, the angels and demons who often walked on earth, constantly assaulting or assisting humans, do not belong to this collection of essentially human beings, although some of those included are legendary and mythical. I have not included giants, elves and other fantastic beings of human appearance, almost none of whom became distinguished enough to become an individualized element that the Middle Ages bequeathed to posterity. We encounter them almost everywhere in the medieval imaginary, but the memory of those beings of exceptional size was not maintained on an individual basis. Among elves, only Oberon with his magic horn, the elf of great beauty in the *chanson de geste Huon de Bordeaux*, has left a trace in musical history thanks to Weber's Romantic opera *Oberon*. The only giant, besides the evil Morholt in the story of Tristan and Iseult, who managed to become a positive hero did so by becoming a saint: St Christopher, who carries the Christ Child on his shoulders in the contemporary imaginary.

By contrast, we will see among the heroes and marvels two representatives from the world of marvellous animals.[7] Animals not only intensely populated the domestic and wild environments of the men and women of the Middle Ages, but assaulted or enlightened their imaginary universe. They are represented here by an imaginary animal, the unicorn, and a real animal, the fox, which became legendary through literature. They illustrate here once again, having been put on the same footing by the men and women of the Middle Ages, the absence of borders between the purely imaginary world and the world transformed into fantasy that characterized the medieval universe, which ignored any demarcation between the natural and the supernatural, the here below and the beyond, reality and fantasy. We will not, however, encounter an essential member of the herd of imaginary animals: monsters.[8] Monsters were usually purely evil beings, and the heroes and marvels in this work are either positive or at least ambiguous. It is the best of the medieval imaginary that is presented here.

The other category in this book, along with heroes, is marvels.[9] The marvellous is a category bequeathed by antiquity, and more specifically by Roman scholarship, to the Christian Middle Ages. The term, which appears primarily in the form of *mirabilia*, in the plural, describes astonishing geographical, and more generally natural, realities. The notion invaded medieval literature and sensibility through the vulgate in various languages: *merveille* is found as early as the thirteenth century in Old French in the *Vie de saint Alexis* and the *Chanson de Roland*; other terms that came out of Latin on the same model are found in Italian, Spanish and Portuguese; in the same period German offered *Wunder* and English *Wonder*, and the Slavic languages such as Polish used the term *Cud*. The marvellous formed a system along with the miraculous and the magical.

The miraculous was reserved for God, and was manifest by a divine act defying the laws of nature. Magic, even if there was a lawful form of white magic, was essentially a condemnable form of witchcraft attributable either to the enemy of humankind, the Devil, or to his henchmen, demons and wizards. But the marvellous, amazing and incomprehensible belongs to the order of nature. In his *Otia imperialia*, the encyclopedia written for Emperor Otto IV around 1210, the Englishman Gervase of Tilbury defines the marvellous as 'That which escapes our understanding, although it is natural'. The category of the marvellous continued to expand during the Middle Ages, because it caused beauties that were somehow taken from God by the industry of men to enter into the terrestrial and human domain.

The realm of the marvellous is that of the astonishment of the men and women of the Middle Ages. It aroused wonder. It was associated with vision, the most exercised and most praised of the senses of medieval man. The marvellous opened the eyes of the men and women of the Middle Ages, while at the same time exciting their minds and spirits. The marvellous is portrayed in this work through three structures, each of which is devoted to one of the three main powers that dominated and directed medieval society. The first of these was God and his priests, and the marvel was the cathedral. The second was the feudal lord, and the marvel was the fortified castle. The third was monastic society, and the marvel was the cloisters.

Each of these structures enveloped a marvellous enclosed space. Thus they were reminders of the enclosed garden and of paradise, marvellous spatial territories.

The medieval imaginary was obviously linked to space and time. From the perspective of space, it was basically European. Although in some cases the hero or marvel was linked to a specific part of Christendom, though not confined to it, such as Arthur and Robin Hood, who are mainly British, and El Cid, who is mainly Spanish, Melusina filled the dreams of people in France and Cyprus, which was ruled by the house of Lusignan for nearly three centuries, and the Valkyrie was found in both Germanic and Scandinavian countries.

From a chronological point of view, I have chosen to present the imaginary that was created and modelled by the Middle Ages, so I have neglected what came from Graeco-Roman antiquity or from Asia. In the chapter 'Knights and Chivalry', as regards the *preux*, we will see how men in the fourteenth century, in addition to illustrious figures from the Middle Ages, turned three ancient figures – Hector, Alexander and Caesar – and three biblical figures – Joshua, David and Judas Maccabee – into *preux*. We will not find these *preux*, who were simply borrowed by the Middle Ages, in this book. After some hesitation, I also excluded Alexander, who was extremely popular in the medieval imaginary but was not created by it. Likewise, I did not include biblical heroes who were not invented by the Middle Ages and were generally transformed by medieval clerics into something other than heroes or *preux*, with the exception of biblical *preux* from the concept of nine *preux* or the Nine Worthies. If David's reputation lived on in the Middle Ages, it was as a king and musician. If Solomon had a troubled history during the medieval period, going from the image of an evil wizard to that of a blessed sage, he does not fit within the problematics of heroes and marvels.

In the margins of the marvellous world there are, it seems to me, only two biblical candidates for inclusion: one Old Testament figure, Jonah, who was marvellously swallowed and spat out by a whale; and the universe of fearsome marvels that Christianity included in the New Testament, but which despite their success remained foreign to it – the heroes and monstrous marvels of the Apocalypse.

The 'Orient', and more specifically India, was one of the great sources of the medieval imaginary.[10] But only one Indian hero, the priest John – a Christian, moreover – stood out individually in the medieval West. He was a twelfth-century king-priest who was believed to have sent a letter to Westerners in which he describes the marvels of India. However, this text circulated only within scholarly circles, and the priest John did not become popular enough to be included among the heroes and marvels of the medieval West.

This particular dissemination of myths is closely related to the history of civilizations. The focus of this book is the realm of medieval Christian culture and the sources it inherited: the Bible, Graeco-Roman antiquity, and Celtic, Germanic and mainly Slavic pagan traditions. Its broad social diffusion made it a realm that was shared by what was called the scholarly and the 'popular' cultures. And so, we will often be led to delve into European and international folklore and to cite distant sources or cultural communities, especially that which is called Indo-European (as mentioned, for example, in the chapters on Arthur and Melusina). But, without denying any kinships or associations, we have above all stressed the creative force of the medieval West in the realm of the imaginary as in all realms of civilization, and the originality of most of its creations. The datable creation of the utopia of the Land of Cockaigne is a good example of this. To take the example of a collective hero, the knight, who was very present in this imaginary, can medieval knights be reduced to heroes of the Indo-European second function, to the Roman *equites*, to Japanese samurai? And wasn't the chivalrous spirit a creation and legacy of the European Middle Ages?

Similarly, a myth is usually linked to a place or to a specific space; the Western Middle Ages attached its heroes and marvels to places, even if they were not their places of origin, and gave them a significant geographical anchoring – whether or not the geography was real or imaginary.

From a chronological point of view, too, this imaginary was formed throughout the Middle Ages, from the fourth to the fourteenth centuries. But it flourished primarily, and essentially turned into a more or less coherent universe, in the great period of the medieval West that not only witnessed its rise, but, as I have tried to demonstrate, brought the values and images of heaven down to Earth. The heroes and marvels of the Middle Ages were beacons, the prowess of that settlement of Christians on an Earth that they embellished with elements enhancing the glory and charm of the supernatural world. Just as the heavenly Jerusalem had descended from heaven to Earth, the heroes and marvels generated and created by God were welcomed and exalted by humans here below. I hope that this book will illustrate that great movement of conversion to the here below of the Christians of the Middle Ages within a context of legends and myths.[11]

This history of the imaginary is also to a large extent an in-depth history of the *longue durée*. It presents medieval heroes and marvels the way the Middle Ages constructed, revered, loved and then bequeathed them to future centuries, where they continued to live by transforming themselves into a combination of reference to the past, adaptation to the present, and an opening to the future. In a certain sense, it is a history of attitudes towards the Middle Ages, of the *Goût du Moyen Âge* (Taste for the Middle Ages), to borrow the title of a wonderful book by Christian Amalvi.

This book is an extension within the field of the imaginary of my work *L'Europe est-elle née au Moyen Âge?*[12] The reader will see that although the essential foundations of Europe have endured since the Middle Ages, the legacy of myths, heroes and marvels faded or was 'lost' in the seventeenth and eighteenth centuries, a period during which a 'dark' image of the Middle Ages was formed and strengthened, from humanism to the Enlightenment; it was seen as a time of darkness, a world of shadows, the Dark Ages. With some exceptions, the heroes and marvels of the Middle Ages became 'barbaric' again – the evolution of the Gothic linked to the cathedral was exemplary in this regard – or, even worse, were covered with a forgetful dismissal similar to the plaster and lime that concealed medieval frescoes.

Romanticism, however, brought back to life the legends and myths of the Middle Ages, made them live again in the imaginary, made them a golden legend. This book aims to illustrate the avatars of memory, the eclipses and resurrections, the transfigurations of a civilization through that which is most brilliant, most brilliantly emblematic, within it.

Following these metamorphoses of the medieval imaginary up to the present demonstrates the way in which the heroes and marvels have been illuminated with a light that restores their 'truth' without removing the mystical aura that explains their success and their historical function. Today, the Middle Ages are popular, situated between shadow and light.[13] I hope to contribute to the popularity of the 'nouveau' Middle Ages, to show where it came from, what it is and what its future, both European and globalized, may be.

To do so, this work presents the reader with paths rather than data; it also reveals the fact that history, created from documents that nourish techniques for resurrecting the past, changes and is transformed through the invention of new means of expression and communication, such as the substitution of the written word for the oral tradition in the Middle Ages. We will see that after its rebirth with Romanticism, a third revival of the medieval imaginary occurred through two major inventions of the twentieth century: film and comics.[14] If there is a field of history that is profoundly perpetuated and renewed through the great waves of revolutions in texts and images, it is indeed the history of the imaginary.

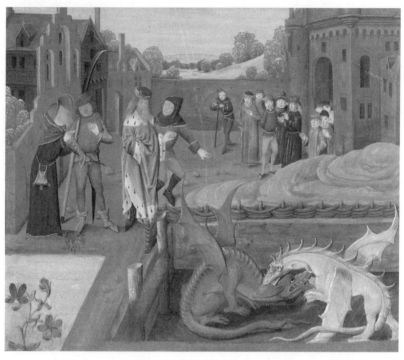

King Arthur and Merlin the Enchanter look on while red and white dragons battle. Illustration from the *St Albans Chronicle*, 15th century.

ARTHUR

Arthur is an exemplary hero of the Middle Ages. Though his legend may have been inspired by a real man, we know almost nothing about that person.

Arthur is one of those medieval heroes who, existing between reality and the imaginary, between history and fiction, evolved into mythical figures, similar to actual historical figures who passed beyond the realm of history to become myths and join fictional heroes in the world of the medieval imaginary. We will meet two such heroes, Arthur and Charlemagne, whose mythical evolutions between history and myth were sometimes parallel and sometimes intersected.

Arthur appeared in the early ninth century in the *Historia Brittonum* (History of the Britons) by the chronicler Nennius, who records that a certain Arthur fought against the Saxons alongside the king of the Britons during the Saxon invasion of Britain. A great warrior, he was said to have killed up to 960 enemies. And so, Arthur entered history as an exceptional warrior, as a defender of the Britons, and in the High Middle Ages his aura remained associated with Celtic oral literature, in particular in the Welsh *Mabinogion*, which recounts the hero's childhood. Arthur has been connected to heroes from other cultures, and in particular to the trifunctional culture of the Indo-Europeans, or to European and even Germanic folklore. But, whatever the background of the hero Arthur, the one that the Western Middle Ages created and bequeathed to us was a Celtic hero specifically associated with British national ideology.

Arthur truly came onto the scene in the *Historia regum Britanniae* (History of the Kings of Britain), written between 1135 and 1138 by Geoffrey of Monmouth, a chronicler probably of Welsh birth and a secular canon in Oxford. Geoffrey tells the story of the kings of Britain starting with Brutus, one of the Romans who brought to the Britons their first taste of civilization. An amalgam of Romans and barbarians, the Britons were governed by a series of kings, the last of whom, Uther Pendragon, aided by the spells of the wizard Merlin, sired a son, Arthur, with his beloved Igraine. King at the age of fifteen, Arthur won battle after battle over the Romans and other tribes of Western Europe. He conquered all of Great Britain, the northern islands and the Continent down to the Pyrenees after killing the giant who was wreaking havoc around Mont Saint-Michel. But his nephew Mordred stole his wife and his kingdom. Returning from battle, Arthur killed him, but he was also supposedly fatally wounded and was transported to the Isle of Avalon off the coast of Wales, where he would either die or convalesce in order to regain his kingdom and empire. Arthur quickly became the central hero of a body of literary texts, the Arthurian legend, which became one of the richest and most enduring creations of the medieval imaginary.

The essential elements of this literary creation can be found in the romances of Chrétien de Troyes, written between 1160 and 1185, and in the Arthurian legend in prose of the first half of the thirteenth century. These works reveal just how much the creative imagination of medieval writers was a driving force in the construction of the heroes and marvels of the medieval imaginary. In studying the history of the imaginary we are able to discover the important place medieval literature held in the culture, mentality and ideology of the time, and its continued importance throughout the centuries. Arthur is the central figure of the great literary field that has been called the 'Matter of Britain'. He inspired the creation of, or gathered around him, a whole series of other heroes, the most spectacular of whom were Gawain, Lancelot and Perceval. He created that utopian institution, one of the few in the medieval Christian West, the Round Table, whose knights were exemplary heroes, as will be seen in the chapter 'Knights and Chivalry'. Arthur is also the link between the hero warrior (his own role) and Merlin, the one who accompanies him from birth to death with his prophecies and protection. Arthur is present at the birth of an extraordinary marvel, the Holy Grail, which is not included in this book because it has practically disappeared from the contemporary imaginary. The Grail was a magical object that became a sort of ciborium, the quest for and conquest of which was demanded of Christian knights, in particular those of the Round Table. It was the myth that culminated in the chivalrous Christianization of the Middle Ages. The utopia of the Round Table allows us to see that the world of heroes and marvels also concealed the contradictions of medieval society and culture. The Round Table was the dream of a world of equality that did not exist in medieval society, which was extremely hierarchical and not at all egalitarian. Yet in feudal ideology there was an aspiration within the upper echelons, among the nobles and aristocrats, to create institutions and encourage behaviour promoting equality. The kiss on the mouth exchanged by the lord and his vassal is a symbolic gesture of this. The Round Table, in addition to its reference to the global nature of the universe, to the whole globe, was a dream of equality of which Arthur was the guarantor, and which would find its social embodiment in the aristocratic world.

Even more than a warrior and a knight, however, Arthur was the mythical embodiment of the leader par excellence of the medieval political world: he was the king. It is significant that very early on, as seen, for example, in the mid-twelfth-century mosaic floor of the cathedral of Santa Maria Annunziata in Otranto, southern Italy, Arthur's full name was *Rex Arturus*. Arthur remains in the European poetic imaginary the symbol of that king who now exists only in a profoundly de-mythicized form, without having completely lost his sacral nature. Arthur was a king who was not only both present and mythical, but millennial. The men and women of the Middle Ages often dreamed of the emergence on earth of a reign of Faith and Virtue, of an apocalyptic millennium led by a king who returned from history. This theme, known as the 'hidden emir', was very popular in Asia. In the West his role was assumed by emperors such as Frederick Barbarossa (who, as the story went, did not die but was sleeping in a cave), and especially by Arthur, who was waiting to return from Avalon. The theme was summed up by *Rex quondam, rexque futurus* – the Once and Future King.

In addition to the Round Table, the mythical object closely associated with Arthur's image, there is another personal object, one of great importance to warriors and knights, that is even more closely connected to his name – his sword. It is a magical sword whose weight only he could handle, and with which he skilfully killed enemies and monsters, particularly giants. And when he threw it into the lake, that gesture announced the end of his life and his power. The sword is called Excalibur. Its disappearance is the beginning of the end of Arthur, which the great British film-maker John Boorman recounts in his film *Excalibur* (1981). We will also encounter personalized swords at the sides of Charlemagne and Roland; Joyeuse, Durandal and Excalibur were the marvellous companions of exceptional heroes. Arthur is foremost the embodiment of a combination of values developed in the Middle Ages that, while strongly marked with a Christian imprint, were above all secular values upheld by lay heroes. Arthur embodied the two successive periods of feudal values: prowess in the twelfth century and courtliness in the thirteenth. He was the trifunctional king of the Indo-European tradition: the sacred king of the first function, warrior king of the second and civilizing king of the third. He illustrated what the great historian of medieval literature, Erich Köhler, defined very well: 'The dual project of the feudal courtly world: historical legitimation and the development of myths.'

Like all heroes, especially those of the Middle Ages, Arthur is closely linked to places. These were places of battle, residence and death. First, there was the region where most of his battles,

Arthur presides over the Round Table with the Holy Grail in the centre. Only nine knights are depicted with him. Manuscript from Paris, 14th century.

conquests and victories took place – the Celtic lands: Ireland, Wales, Cornwall and Armorica. Here were Tintagel in Cornwall, where it was believed Arthur was conceived, while Camelot, Arthur's imaginary capital, was early associated with Caerleon in Wales.[1] Between these sites lay marvellous islands such as Avalon. It was at the Benedictine abbey of Glastonbury in Somerset, however, where his remains and those of Queen Guinevere were believed to have been found in 1191. But far from the Celtic world there is also an amazing place between life and death connected to Arthur, the king in waiting. This place is Etna, where it was believed that Arthur was taken, far from all suffering, as told in an astonishing collection of marvellous tales by the Englishman Gervase of Tilbury in the early thirteenth century. Arthur was waiting, at rest and peaceful, either for a marvellous return to earth or for his sublimation into paradise. And so Arthur is connected to what I have called the birth of purgatory, to a moment in time when rulers hesitated between Ireland and Sicily, and when the Celtic king became one of the first inhabitants of that purgatory that so consumed Christendom.[2]

But in Christian Europe – and this fact has remained true to the present day – there was no all-powerful hero or marvel that did not have a flipside. The hero was only a man, and every man was a sinner, and in a feudal society based on fidelity there were inevitably contrasting moments of betrayal by the wicked. Furthermore, if monarchical ideology turned the king's character into that of a hero, it was far from granting him the absolutist nature that the Renaissance and the classical era attributed to him. Arthur was a sinner, Arthur was betrayed. Arthur, defeated by concupiscence, slept with his sister, and out of that incest Mordred was born. For every great figure there is great sin: kings and heroes, like Charlemagne, are often incestuous. As for the fruit of the sin, Mordred, he was the traitor whose death led to that of the king; and if Arthur experienced another betrayal, that of his wife Guinevere, who slept with his vassal Lancelot, Arthur himself on various occasions betrayed Guinevere.

Arthur's popularity continued to grow in the years following Geoffrey of Monmouth. It was initially ensured by the policies of the Plantagenet kings of England. Using heroes in politics has been widely seen throughout history, especially in the Middle Ages, and throughout European history. Furthermore, the kings of England exalted Arthur when they were confronted with the Germans and the French, who in this race for historic-mythical sponsorship were seeking increasingly to monopolize Charlemagne. So throughout the history of Europe, Arthur and Charlemagne, a duo each with two sides, came into play, sometimes reinforcing each other, sometimes in opposition.

Arthur's popularity was so great that at the beginning of the thirteenth century, the Cistercian prior Caesarius of Heisterbach wrote in his *Dialogus miraculorum* that once the monks were dozing during their abbot's sermon when all of a sudden he raised his voice: 'Listen to me, my brothers, listen well, I am going to tell you a new and extraordinary fact: there was once a king named Arthur.' Upon those words the monks stirred, woke up and were all ears. Arthur had become a hero even in the cloister. Another testimony to the success of Arthur's image in medieval society, far beyond aristocratic circles, is the popularity of the name Arthur, which can be found at the moment when modern anthroponymy, which attached a surname to a first name, notably within urban social milieus, was formed in the thirteenth- and fourteenth-century Christian West. Michel Pastoureau has admirably revealed the diffusion of the first name Arthur, and of first names drawn from the names of the leading

Knights of the Round Table, pointing out that a baptismal name is never neutral, that it is 'the first social marker, the first attribute, the first emblem'. He studied the frequency of the names of the Knights of the Round Table from around 40,000 inscriptions on French official seals from before the end of the fifteenth century. They show that 'playing King Arthur' had become an authentic urban fact: a true Arthurian frenzy had developed in certain regions such as the Netherlands and Italy, up to the middle of the sixteenth century. Back in France, the winner of this anthroponymic competition was Tristan, with 120 examples, followed by Lancelot with 79 mentions. But Arthur was very close with 72 examples, far ahead of Gawain (46) and Perceval (44).

As will often be seen in this book, the prestigious heroes of the Middle Ages, who often lay more or less dormant in the fourteenth century, woke up in the fifteenth, which, as Johan Huizinga has superbly shown in *The Waning of the Middle Ages* (1919), was a century that had succumbed to the most exuberant interest in chivalry. An English poet, Sir Thomas Malory, woke Arthur up in his great poem *Le Morte d'Arthur*, published in 1485. The sixteenth century preserved the enchanted memory of this medieval hero so well that another poet, Edmund Spenser, brought Arthur back to life again in *The Faerie Queen* (1590). Borne by British nationalism, Arthur travelled through the seventeenth-century imaginary rather well. This was due primarily to the work of the great musician Henry Purcell, who composed his semi-opera *King Arthur; or, The British Worthy* with a libretto by the equally great poet John Dryden, who revised an earlier version of the story of Arthur, written for King Charles II, into a popular commercial success in 1691.

Later, Arthur was part of a great revival of the medieval imaginary with the advent of Romanticism. He became the hero of one of

Knight from the King Arthur parody film *Monty Python and the Holy Grail* (dir. Terry Gilliam and Terry Jones, 1975).

the greatest English Romantic poets, Alfred, Lord Tennyson, who in 1842 published *The Passing of Arthur* and who continued to work on *Idylls of the King* (1885) until his death. At about the same time, Arthur was also reborn in the works of the Pre-Raphaelite painters, primarily Dante Gabriel Rossetti (1828–1882) and Edward Burne-Jones (1833–1898). In music, Ernest Chausson, under the influence of Richard Wagner, who played a decisive role in the rebirth of heroes and marvels (mainly Germanic) of the medieval imaginary, composed his only opera, *Le roi Arthus*, between 1886 and 1895.

Finally, the world of film revived the prestige of the medieval hero Arthur and of his principal heroic companions. Jean Cocteau began by bringing the Arthurian legend to the stage with his play *Les Chevaliers de la Table ronde* (1937). After the war, film masterpieces and others that were more or less distorted by the views of the Middle Ages that proliferated among audiences through cinematographic productions, offered spectacular works such as Hollywood's *Knights of the Round Table* (dir. Richard Thorpe; 1953) and Lerner and Loewe's musical *Camelot* (dir. Joshua Logan, 1967). The great works are *Lancelot du Lac* (Lancelot of the Lake) (dir. Robert Bresson, 1974), *Perceval le Gallois* (Perceval) (dir. Eric Rohmer, 1978) and *Excalibur* (dir. John Boorman, 1981). In *Indiana Jones and the Last Crusade* (1989), Steven Spielberg launches Harrison Ford in search of the Holy Grail. Parody, also a sign of popularity, has made us laugh at Arthur in *Monty Python and the Holy Grail* (dir. Terry Gilliam and Terry Jones, 1975), with its stage musical spin-off by Eric Idle, *Spamalot* (2004), and the various adaptations of Mark Twain's novel *A Connecticut Yankee in King Arthur's Court* (1899), including a 1949 musical (dir. Tay Garnett) starring Bing Crosby. The ultra-conservative Hollywood producer Jerry Bruckheimer provided a sumptuous budget for the spectacular *King Arthur* (dir. Antoine Fuqua, 2004), in which Arthur, Guinevere and the Knights of the Round Table are portrayed as heroes of a Britain intent on fighting the Saxons after the end of the Roman occupation to enable the country to continue on the road to progress. Fuqua has noted that in the film there are echoes between how Britain had to free itself from its Roman past to accomplish its civilizing mission and fight against barbarism, and the situation in Afghanistan and Iraq. Arthur is not done surprising us.

THE CASTLE

The 'marvellous' monuments of the Middle Ages that have left a mythical image in the European imaginary are primarily the cathedral and the castle. The type of castle that became a mythical structure in medieval society and for European civilization is the fortified castle. The term *château fort* appeared only in 1835 during the Romantic revival of the medieval imaginary.

Since the Middle Ages a castle has sometimes been confused with a palace, but they were two distinct entities within the history of reality and myth. A palace had two specific characteristics that distinguished it from a castle. First, it was essentially a royal residence, or at least a princely one, whereas a castle was that of a mere lord, even though kings, as lords, were known to build castles. Of the two essential functions of a castle – military defence and residence – it was mainly the second function that predominated in a palace, whereas a castle was foremost meant for fortified defence.

Castles are closely connected to feudalism, and their recurring image in the European imaginary attests to the fact that in the feudal system, and in the period from the tenth century to the French Revolution as a whole, castles were fundamental elements in the material, social and symbolic realities of Europe. Overall, we can detect a slow but continual evolution of castles from their role as

Pierre le Baud, 'The Fight of the Thirty in 1351', from the
Chronicle of Brittany, 15th century.

fortress to that of residence. As castles were closely associated with military activity, it is notable that their transformation was decisively triggered by the technical revolution in artillery in the fourteenth and fifteenth centuries. Castle walls no longer held up to cannon fire, and castles remained as relics, symbols, ruins, and, for many, evoked nostalgia. For the whole period of the Middle Ages that concerns us here, however, we might describe a castle as 'an inhabited fortress'.

From the tenth century to the twelfth, castles first appeared in two forms. In northern Europe these were towers and modest fortified settlements built on natural or artificial mounds, known as *châteaux sur motte* (castles on a hill). In southern Europe the early castles, called *roques*, were more commonly built on natural rocky heights. Contrary to what has sometimes been written, castles on hills and *roques* were not built primarily of wood; rather, from the beginning castles were made of stone and proved, as did cathedrals, that there had been a return to and promotion of stone in the Middle Ages. In general, castles, like religious houses, were not separated from the natural environment. Castles rooted feudalism on the rural ground, unlike cathedrals, which were integrated and dominant in cities and in which nature was evoked only when the Romantic imaginary turned them into something akin to a forest. As for castles, even if they were built in cities in certain regions of Europe, such as Normandy (Caen), Flanders (Ghent), and especially in Italy, they remained associated with the countryside and even more so with nature. Castles were an element of the spatial network of habitations created by feudalism, both in reality and in the European imaginary.

The increasing number of castles built on hills in the eleventh and twelfth centuries led to the construction of fortresses that would remain emblematic of all castles in the European imaginary.

Such a castle was a donjon, or stronghold (donjon comes from *dominionem*, a seigneurial place), the etymology of which indicates exactly what the castle was: a centre of command. The right to build fortifications, and consequently to construct a castle, was a royal privilege. One of the characteristics of feudalism, however, was the nobility's desire to dispossess kings of their privileges in favour of nobles. The castellans to whom the kings had first entrusted castles quickly became their masters. The resulting attempts by kings and princes to regain control of these castles continued during the feudal era, after the period of what Georges Duby has called *châtellenies indépendantes* (independent lordships) from the beginning of the eleventh century to the middle of the twelfth. Dukes of Normandy, kings of England, counts of Barcelona and kings of Aragon regained control over the castles of their nobles rather easily, but the struggles of the first Capetian kings against the castellans of the Île-de-France in the eleventh and twelfth centuries were long and difficult.

Initially appearing above all in border areas and conflict zones, castles were soon found throughout Christendom. Thus dozens of castles were constructed in Catalonia in the tenth century to counter the threat from the Moors, and Castile owes its name to them. As feudalism developed, fortified villages, or castles in which all or some of the inhabitants of the seigneury resided, began to appear. Pierre Toubert, who studied the phenomenon in the Latium region of Italy, proposed the term *incastellamento*, which became one of the jewels in the vocabulary of medieval feudalism. Although castles were built everywhere from the eleventh to the sixteenth centuries, certain regions had particularly large numbers, due notably to military conflicts and feudal settlements in the area. In the thirteenth century, for example, Wales, which was claimed by the English, was covered with castles, while Spain remained a region teeming with castles, as the Christian rulers of the *Reconquista* promised either existing castles or those still to be built to warriors who followed them into battle. This is the origin of the expression *chateâux en Espagne* or 'castles in Spain', meaning 'castles in the air', which further rooted castles in the dreams of Christian Europe.

Either in their own time, or in the modern and contemporary imaginary, some castles acquired an impressive aura. Without the spirituality of cathedrals, castles proclaimed their symbolic power and imposed themselves as the source of strength and power. As an example, during one of the first big clashes between Christian nations, the twelfth-century rivalry between France and England, the fortress of Château-Gaillard was built by King Richard I of England (the Lionheart) in 1197–8 at the heart of the French territory disputed by the English. Its location overlooking a bend in the Seine highlights the castle's spectacular connection to its environment.

Around 1240, Frederick II, emperor of Germany and king of Sicily, had the Castel del Monte built in Apulia. Through its design and ornamentation, Frederick II made this octagonal castle a masterpiece combining the great Christian and Islamic architectural traditions of its time.

The Château de Coucy, which Count Enguerrand III had rebuilt between 1225 and 1245, is commonly considered a perfect example of a medieval castle. Here is how an archaeologist describes it:

> It is indeed a fortress of that time, and among the most impressive, with its trapezoidal layout, its four corner towers, its huge donjon towering over the longest façade, totally separate from the curtain, and even in its deep interior ditch:

its dimensions make it a formidable fortress: walls six metres high, towers forty metres high, a donjon 55 metres high and 31 metres in diameter.[1]

Though a castle built in a natural environment is the model of the feudal castle par excellence, there are nonetheless prestigious examples of urban castles. In Paris, opposite the royal residence of the Palais de la Cité, the Capetian kings from 1190 built a fortress, the Louvre, on the north bank of the Seine. After the city wall was extended in the mid-fourteenth century this too became a royal residence. A fortification built to protect the gateway at the eastern edge of city was used as a royal prison from the reign of Louis XI (r. 1461–83) and became the symbol of the tyrannical castle: the Bastille. The French Revolution began with the taking and destruction of a castle.

The dukes of Normandy, later kings of England, built castles as residences both, for example, at Caen – where outstanding excavations led by Michel de Boüard in the second half of the twentieth century established the contemporary study of castles, castellology – and in their English capital, where the Tower of London, built by William the Conqueror after 1077, is an illustrious example of an urban castle. In Rome the Pope, the most prestigious sovereign in Italy, although not always the most obeyed, employed the concept of 're-use' to change the huge tomb of Emperor Hadrian (d. AD 138) into first a fortress and then, from the late fourteenth century, a fortified private residence, the Castel Sant'Angelo. When the popes left Rome for Avignon in the fourteenth century, they had one of the most spectacular castles built there, a residence that, despite its name, the Palais des Papes, was really more of a fortress. In Florence the great families, beginning with the Medicis, built more palaces than castles, while in fifteenth-century Milan the Sforzas built a fortress-residence, the Castello Sforzesco, which retained the image and role of a castle.

Castles continued to evolve, as described by Pierre Bonnassie:

> The first donjons were very cramped and uncomfortable, they most often consisted of only one sitting and reception room (*aula*) and a bedroom (*camara*), where the castellan and his entire '*mesnie*' (family and vassals) all slept together. But the setting for seigneurial life expanded quickly with the new wealth made possible through economic growth. In the twelfth and thirteenth centuries the castellan was in a position to practise widely that cardinal virtue of the time: generosity [rather, largesse]. Parties began to be held in the fortress, which became the acknowledged place for the good life: the castle henceforth became the setting for the courtly civilization.[2]

That is when what has been called 'castle life' began to flourish; alongside the functions of power and defence, castle life henceforth encompassed 'customs, a culture, a lifestyle of opulence and pleasure'.

The fourteenth century saw the widespread construction of drawbridges, the replacement of wooden hoarding with stone machicolation supported on corbels, an increase in inner and outer curtain walls and barbicans, and, in the large and new royal fortresses, a continuous defensive line along the top of towers and curtain walls, forming a vast terrace, as can be seen on engravings of the Bastille and the castle at Tarascon completed by René I of Anjou in 1447–9. Though there still wasn't much furniture inside, the walls began to be covered with increasingly elaborate textiles;

cushions and fabric window panes were added, as were curtains and wall hangings. According to Jean-Marie Pesez,

> the castle of the late Middle Ages was more open to the outside, and the rooms were lighted by day through real windows, which were often simply covered with latticework, but sometimes had glass or at least paper or oiled canvas; on either side of the window, window seats, stone benches built right into the wall, created a more sociable intimate space than did the vast halls.

With machicolations and other fanciful architectural elements, the castle's mythical image was enhanced even more.

Castles continued to be built throughout Christendom, for example, in Poland. Malbork Castle, built in the thirteenth century by the Knights of the Teutonic Order, became one of the new urban castles of the kings of Poland. In the fifteenth century Wawel Castle was built next to the cathedral on the hill overlooking Kraków. It was not until 1611 that the king of Poland, having transferred the capital from Kraków to Warsaw, built a Royal Castle in Warsaw which, despite its clearly having been a residence, retains the appearance of a fortress. The original structure was destroyed by the Germans during the Second World War, but the post-war Communist regime ultimately decided to rebuild it during the 1970s, both as an attempt to be reconciled with the Polish population and, above all, as a sign of the renaissance of the Polish nation. The great Polish historian Aleksander Gieysztor was asked to direct the restoration. Thus at the end of the twentieth century, in its trajectory within the historical imaginary, the castle, like the cathedral, also became a national symbol.

Illuminated page from the *Très riches heures du duc de Berry*,
15th century, featuring an image of the Château de Mehun-sur-Yèvre.

The castle of the fifteenth century, long associated with festivals, became a real theatrical venue, a theatre of life or of the world (*theatrum vitae* or *theatrum mundi*). Here again, taking the place of the theatre, which would come back to life only belatedly and with difficulty, the cathedral and the castle became theatrical spaces in the period between antiquity and the modern era. The most complete and most refined model of the royal castle at the end of the Middle Ages is without doubt the one in Mehun-sur-Yèvre, which is almost completely in ruins today, but whose mythicized image we can see in the miniatures of the *Très riches heures du duc de Berry* from the beginning of the fifteenth century:

> A castle in its low parts, the sloping of its towers, its false braies,[3] the austerity of its walls, the width of its moats, in its upper sections it displays all the refinements of the late Gothic: skylights, gables bristling with the pinnacles of turrets, corbels, with a huge stone knight six metres high standing in the gable of the reception hall, the great hall, and sculptures everywhere, enamelled tiles, with the emblems of the duke, Jean de Berry: the lily, the bear, the wounded swan.[4]

The castle of Mehun-sur-Yèvre is a fairy-tale castle that materializes the dreams that have been inspired by castles ever since the eleventh century.

Between their abandonment due to their inability to resist artillery or to their lack of comfort, and their destruction by kings and others eager to destroy feudalism, such as Louis XIII and Richelieu, castles drifted into a phase of neglect in the seventeenth and eighteenth centuries. Looking at images of castles in eighteenth-century dictionaries shows that during the Enlightenment the castle became a retrograde and rustic image of feudalism.[5]

The castle was, of course, resurrected by Romanticism. Victor Hugo, travelling on the Rhine, was moved by the nostalgic silhouette of the castles he encountered, while the movement of the Restoration, which in the same period caused German nationalist Romanticism to resume work on Cologne Cathedral, led to a rebuilding, often in fantastical styles, of the castles that embellish the Middle Rhine Valley. Schloss Stolzenfels, near Koblenz, was built by Archbishop Arnold von Isenburg (1241–59) but destroyed by the army of Louis XIV in 1688. In 1802 the city of Koblenz offered the ruins to the Crown Prince of Prussia, the future Friedrich Wilhelm IV. He entrusted the reconstruction to the architect Karl Friedrich Schinkel, who carried it out starting in 1836. It is a blend of Romantic medievalism and the bourgeois Biedermeier spirit of the nineteenth century. The reconstruction enhanced the castle's theatrical aspect; it was, moreover, intended to be a theatre for royal performances, bringing together nature and built structures. The interior decor exalts medieval chivalry with historical paintings, weapons and armour.[6]

Other castles were wonderfully reconstructed through the initiatives of royal rulers in the second half of the nineteenth century. In France, Viollet-le-Duc restored for Emperor Napoleon III and Empress Eugénie the château at Pierrefonds, built at the beginning of the fifteenth century for Louis d'Orléans, which had fallen into ruins. The restored Pierrefonds, along with a renewed exaltation of the medieval *preux*, became exemplary of a rebirth of sensibilities and medieval symbolism. It was not by chance that the same great architect was responsible for resurrecting both Notre-Dame de Paris and Pierrefonds.

Another even more spectacular example of this is the series of amazing castles with a 'Middle Ages' character built for Ludwig II of Bavaria (r. 1864–86), the 'Mad King'. The principal ones are the castles of Neuschwanstein, Linderhof, Herrenchiemsee and Hohenschwangau. After he was declared mentally incapable, Ludwig was taken to another of the castles he had improved, Schloss Berg, and was found drowned in the shallows of Lake Starnberg nearby.

With Romanticism, the castle, like the cathedral, became a metaphor. Thus Gérard de Nerval, haunted by castles, sings the praises of the 'soul castle',[7] which probably inspired Rimbaud:

O seasons, O castles
Which soul is flawless?

And Verlaine, imprisoned in Mons, transformed his prison into a 'castle of the soul':

Castle, magical castle,
Where my soul is made.

But the castle could also be a castle of tyranny. Victor Hugo, in *Quatre-vingt-treize*, uses as a model the fortress of La Tourgue in the forest of Fougères. Here the relationship between the castle and nature is one of fear: 'A monster of stone was the counterpart of the wooden monster'. And, summing up this symbolism of the castle of tyranny, Hugo writes:

La Tourgue was this ill-fated result of the past which was called the Bastille in Paris, the Tower of London in England, the Spilberk in Germany, the Escorial in Spain, the Kremlin in Moscow, the Castelo Sant'Angelo in Rome. In La Tourgue were condensed 1,500 years, the Middle Ages, vassalage, serfs, feudalism.

In Polish national literature of the nineteenth century, however, the castle in ruins became the symbol of the castle of glory to be rebuilt, as in Adam Mickiewicz's famous *Pan Tadeusz*, and in his *Grażyna*, a Lithuanian tale that describes the castle of Navahrudak, now in Belarus, as well as in Seweryn Goszczyński's novel *Krol zamczyska* (King of the Castle; 1842). Kórnik Palace, near Poznań, another of Schinkel's designs, is the embodiment of the dream of chivalrous glory, complete with its trophy room and lavish decor, including a Moorish salon.

In the twentieth century and down to the present day, the castle created and bequeathed by feudalism is still present in the European imaginary. In the Middle Ages it had been transplanted to Palestine as a fundamental element of Christendom by the Crusades. The Krak des Chevaliers in Syria has remained a spectacular example of this, despite suffering from shelling and an air strike in the Syrian civil war. It is interesting to discover that one of the most legendary representatives of adventure in the twentieth century, Lawrence of Arabia, wrote his thesis on 'The Influence of the Crusades on European Military Architecture' after sketching and analysing the castles of Syria in 1909, years before he joined military intelligence during the First World War and played an important role in the Arab revolt against the Ottoman forces.

In general, the still present image of the castle in the Western imaginary reminds us that in the medieval period war was omnipresent, and that our heroes, aside from the saints so-called through the grace of God, were warriors who, before they demonstrated their prowess, were distinguished by the nature of their residences, which were closely associated with war.

Another example of the permanence of the castle in the European imaginary is the importance its image has assumed in the sensibilities of children. The castle is the subject of classroom studies and drawings. It fills cartoons, films, television and *son et lumière* extravaganzas. Among medieval marvels, the castle has strengthened its hold on the Western imaginary through its conquest of the minds and sensibilities of children.

THE CATHEDRAL

The cathedral is associated with the first of the three orders of medieval Indo-European society, priests; the castle is associated with the second, warriors. We could add a structure, or rather a grouping of structures, to represent the productive function of the third order, the city. But although the medieval city was quite original, compared to the cities of the ancient, industrial and post-industrial eras, it does not seem to have had an identity sufficiently unique to be included among the marvels presented in this book. We should not forget, however, that for the great majority of men and women in the Middle Ages the city was marvellous and beautiful.

The term 'cathedral' first appeared in the Middle Ages in the form of an adjective: the cathedral church. It became a noun only in the seventeenth century, but in that form it experienced an extraordinary success both in the realm of vocabulary and in that of ideology. 'Cathedral' comes from the Latin *cathedra*, a kind of throne reserved for the bishop. This episcopal throne was one of the essential elements of the interior of the cathedral. So the cathedral was essentially – and this, too, ensured its success – the bishop's church. It is notable that the name for cathedral churches in European languages came from not one, but two Latin words. In England, Spain and France the word is *cathedral* and comes from

Saint-Denis abbey, choir and north transept.

the episcopal *cathedra*. In Germany and Italy, the cathedral is designated by a word that means house, *domus*, which has given *Dom* in German and *duomo* in Italian. In this form a cathedral is the house of God, even more so than the seat of the bishop.

The cathedral achieved its exceptional status primarily through its dimensions. Impressive because it was the most important church in every diocese, and because it was the head of all churches, meant to receive all the faithful, and to visually impose its status upon them, the cathedral stood out foremost through its extraordinary size. The strength of its image is expressed primarily by its powerful exterior, but also by its grandiose interior. In this respect, the cathedral is the best architectural expression of the intimate union of interior and exterior space that is at the heart of medieval spirituality and sensibilities. In the twentieth century, the impressive image of the cathedral was further confirmed through the practice of aerial photography. Viewed close up, far away, from the outside, from the inside or from the sky, the cathedral today is still an extraordinary structure. Skyscrapers, which through their size and, especially, their height are the only buildings to rival cathedrals, obviously do not have, despite the symbolism with which they have been endowed, the spirituality of cathedrals, something that is still palpable today, even for non-believers or for members of non-Christian religious and cultural communities.

The cathedral is a structure in the historical *longue durée*. It appeared in the fourth century and continues to live a double life today: its life as a church, an ongoing place of worship, and its mythical life in the imaginary. The cathedral seems eternal, and yet few buildings have been subjected to as many changes and historical evolutions as it has. And so, the cathedral was born in the fourth century with the recognition of Christianity as the official religion of the Roman Empire, and with the promotion of the bishop among the great figures of power and status.

The cathedral prior to the High Middle Ages, until about the year 1000, was not only the great church that was still known by that name, but a city within a city, a collection of buildings that were called an 'episcopal complex' or 'cathedral complex'. This would usually include two churches, a baptistery, an episcopal palace, a residence for the clergy, a Hôtel-Dieu or hospital and a school. Then the second church disappeared, the baptistery was integrated into the church in the more modest form of baptismal fonts, the clergy's residence became the dwellings of the canons, the Hôtels-Dieu became independent and began competing with hospitals, which proliferated from the twelfth to the thirteenth century, and schools were separated from the cathedral. Cathedral life in the Carolingian period was marked by the introduction of canons into its space, with provision of a residence for them outside, and stalls reserved for their use inside, located in a choir constructed to form, more generally, a physical division between the faithful and the clergy. The choir was hidden from the view of the faithful. Instead of saying mass in front of them, the officiant now turned his back: it had become difficult for the cathedral to play the role of religious and liturgical unifier of the bishop, the canons, the clergy and the mass of the faithful.

The evolution of churches, and in particular of cathedrals, also occurred within the general conditions of historical evolution, in which we can distinguish two great currents. One relates to population growth. The population of the West probably doubled between the year 1000 and the thirteenth century. Furthermore, the space in the cathedral open to the faithful also became a more or less secular collective space, a place for people to meet and socialize, which essentially turned cathedrals into interior forums at a time when urbanization, with which cathedrals were closely associated, was developing exponentially. But I believe that the second historical current, what might be called the architectural 'fashion', was the one that changed the dimensions and appearance of cathedrals the most. Arguing against proponents of functionality as the main driver of historical evolution, one can reasonably emphasize the importance of the role of fashion, which was very obvious from the eleventh and twelfth centuries. In particular, the movement from the Romanesque to the Gothic style was fuelled by changes in taste, and Gothic made it possible to further enhance the original features that had characterized cathedrals since the fourth century.

The Gothic offered cathedrals the triumph of height, enhanced by the increasing numbers and size of windows, especially in the clerestory, to reveal the large interior spaces, and the development of towers and spires that emphasized the primacy of the high over the low, together generating the momentum of elevation that characterized medieval spirituality. Roland Recht has revealed that, rather than an alleged continuity between the Romanesque and the Gothic, Gothic architecture represented a revolutionary breakthrough:

It offered the first radical break with Roman antiquity and the early Christian era, unlike Romanesque architecture which continued that tradition. That break was founded on technical innovations – the invention of intersecting arches supporting the vault, flying buttresses, and the development of stone subframes and thin walls – which gradually enabled structures to be increasingly taller, lighter and much brighter. But that's not all. Gothic architecture also favoured a much richer embellishment, which responded to an increasingly asserted rationality, bringing together each structural element with a determined function. This enrichment conferred a plasticity upon the built structure so that shadow and light engaged in a dialogue of great dramatic intensity. This led to an accentuation of visual effects, an accentuation that accompanied a growing concern with the Incarnation within the Church.[1]

The encounter between the Gothic and the cathedral also occurred under the influence of historical phenomena whose impact is still felt today. The first was the revalorization of the episcopal function under Gregorian reform, which in the second half of the twelfth century removed the Church from the hold of secular feudalism. The second was the greater role of the king in the construction of cathedrals. Building a cathedral became subject to royal approval. From the end of the twelfth century kings exercised this prerogative more carefully, depending on the attention they paid to the construction of what has been called the modern State. Thus cathedrals became associated with States and with burgeoning nations. A monument of a city, the cathedral became a monument of a State.

The Gothic also reinforced a rational aspect in the structure of cathedrals. The German-born American art historian Erwin Panofsky emphasized the parallelism between Gothic cathedrals and scholastic thought. Cathedrals remain even today the major expressions of one of the features of the European mindset, a combination of faith and reason. We should add that the period was also one in which Christianity experienced an increase in wealth, due especially to progress in agriculture and to the marketing of agricultural surpluses. In singing the praises of Chartres, Charles Péguy was right to say of the cathedral: 'It is the sheaf of wheat that will never perish.' And the American art historian Henry Kraus, destroying the fantasy that it was the gifts of materials and work offered by the faithful in the Middle Ages that enabled cathedrals to be constructed without money, has shown that, in his own words, 'gold was the mortar.'

The Gothic also enabled cathedrals to exhibit architectural elements of great significance, such as the portal, and especially the portal of the west facade. The first great example of a cathedral portal that welcomed the faithful was the late twelfth-century Pórtico de la Gloria of Santiago de Compostela Cathedral. Here the salvific function of cathedrals was enhanced by evoking the evangelical declaration of Christ, *Ego sum janua* ('I am the door,' John 10:9), meaning that access to heaven passes through devotion to his person. The eschatological nature of the cathedral was thus emphasized. This could also be found in another element, the labyrinth, many examples of which have unfortunately disappeared due to the post-medieval ignorance of the clergy; the most notable of those that survive is in Chartres Cathedral. Portals also allowed sculpture now to be displayed on the exterior of cathedrals. This exteriorization of sculpture on cathedral portals included the presentation of images of the kings of Judaea and Israel. At Notre-Dame de Paris these were easily assimilated with statues of the kings of France to create a Gallery of Kings across the west facade; some of the heads decapitated during the Revolution were discovered in 1977 in the courtyard of the Hôtel Moreau. The portrayal of history as offered by Christianity, leading up to the Last Judgement, the end of historical time, was here on display for the admiration and edification of the faithful.

We will now look at an issue that has been heatedly debated in the recent past, that of colours in cathedrals. The title of an excellent work by Alain Erlande-Brandenburg, *Quand les cathédrales étaient peintes* (1993),[2] stresses the anachronism of both the exteriors and interiors of cathedrals today. But the frenzied supporters of a return to colours should not forget, when they create often objectionable 'sound and light' extravaganzas, that cathedrals united the colours of the sculptures and tapestries with the force of the divine white light to which they were widely opened.

The great moment of Gothic cathedrals was the period defined by Georges Duby in his seminal work *Le Temps des cathédrales*, which became the basis of a wonderful TV series.[3] The years were 1130–1280, a period during which, according to Duby, 'the horizons of European civilization were profoundly altered'. This period was thus marked by an extraordinary competition in constructing ever larger and taller cathedrals. It is what Jean Gimpel calls 'the world record fever'. Cathedrals exemplified in the Middle Ages what in the twentieth century would be the 'world record fever' in constructing skyscrapers. The largest cathedral was in Amiens, with a surface area of 7,700 square metres built from 1220 to 1269. The vaults of Notre-Dame de Paris, started in 1163, were 35 metres high; Chartres Cathedral, started in 1195, was 36.5 metres high. Reims Cathedral reached 38 metres in 1212 and Amiens 42 metres in 1221. Such excessive heights could lead to disaster: the roof of Troyes Cathedral collapsed in 1228 and the tower of Sens Cathedral fell down in 1267. In a catastrophe that became symbolic, the choir of the Beauvais Cathedral, which had been raised to the greatest height of all, 48 metres, collapsed in 1284.

During this period the Gothic cathedral building movement was particularly active in France, or more precisely in the Île-de-France, to such a degree that the style was sometimes called the 'French art'. Some large French cathedrals indeed served as models for those in southern France or other European regions. After the fire of 1174, Canterbury Cathedral was inspired by that of Sens; in 1220 the elevation of Burgos Cathedral was based on that of Bourges; and after 1248 Cologne Cathedral used Amiens and Beauvais as models. Pope Clement IV, former archbishop of Narbonne, publicly expressed the wish in 1268 that the city's future cathedral would 'imitate' those in the north of the kingdom of France. But the essential point is that cathedrals soon covered all of Europe. In Sweden, Lund Cathedral, built in the twelfth century, retains its Romanesque appearance, but in Roskilde, Denmark, an earlier church was replaced after about 1175 by a brick cathedral that is the earliest in the Baltic region to be influenced by French Gothic. Later, as the burial place of the Danish kings, it became a sort of national cathedral. As the shrine of St Wenceslas, Prague Cathedral had a similar status: the existing building was commissioned in 1342 by the future Emperor Charles IV, who summoned the French master mason Mathias of Arras from Avignon. Gniezno Cathedral, too, housed the major shrine of St Adalbert, and was rebuilt in the Gothic style from 1342 as a Polish national cathedral. In southern Spain, the Christians captured Seville in 1248 and began the long process of converting the city's mosque into the largest church in Christendom, retaining one of its minarets, now known as the Giralda, as the cathedral's bell tower.

The financial crisis of the fourteenth century, which dried up many sources of funding for building cathedrals, left unfinished buildings all over Europe, including cathedrals in Narbonne, Siena and Milan, that embodied unfulfilled dreams and became nostalgic ruins. When the Milanese, for example, considered replacing their cathedral in the mid-fourteenth century, this became the subject of a great debate that focused on which techniques should be used for constructing cathedrals, pitting the brick of the Lombard Gothic tradition against the marble of French master masons, practical know-how against mathematical expertise, and artisanal tradition against academic knowledge. The debate came to exemplify the issues raised by those incomparable monuments.[4] The west facade of Milan Cathedral would remain unfinished until the early nineteenth century.

Before following the lives of cathedrals after the fifteenth century, I should point out that the term 'cathedral' is commonly used today to describe a construction of exceptional size and significance. The term has thus been applied above all to certain constructions of thought and of medieval literary art. Erwin Panofsky saw Thomas Aquinas' *Summa theologica* as a Scholastic cathedral, and Georges Duby held that Dante's *Divine Comedy* was 'a cathedral, the last'.

In the sixteenth century cathedrals became targets of Protestant vandalism, but the Gothic model of the cathedral survived. Orleans Cathedral was destroyed by Protestants in 1568, for example, but was rebuilt in the Gothic style. Furthermore, the Council of Trent initiated a movement that aimed to restore the presence of the laity throughout the cathedral, and to abolish transformations and external constructions that had relegated the faithful to the back of the nave. The cathedral of the Counter-Reformation aimed to express spatially and structurally what had been the great social and symbolic characteristic of the monument: a place of worship and emotion for all, from the bishop down to the meekest of the faithful. Thus, until the beginning of the nineteenth century, chancel screens that hid the choir from the nave were removed, with the exception of those at Auch and Albi. The eighteenth century was a trying period for cathedrals, due to the indifference of 'rationalist' bishops and canons to the imaginary of those monuments. Coats of whitewash covered the colour of the wall paintings, multicoloured stained-glass windows were replaced by panes of frosted glass and labyrinths were destroyed. But the greatest ordeal came during the French Revolution, when cathedrals became the target of revolutionary fervour owing to their connection to royalty, their wealth in accumulated priceless relics and the destruction of the link between faith and reason. The cathedral might become a temple of Reason (in Paris) or of Nature (in Strasbourg), yet, with very few exceptions, no cathedral was destroyed.

The French Revolution adopted the principle applied by Constantine in the fourth century of having administrative districts and ecclesiastical dioceses coincide. Dioceses were now aligned with the new *départements*. The number of cathedrals was reduced to 83. Napoleon reduced the dioceses to 52 in order to keep better watch over the bishops, whom he wanted to make senior government officials reporting to him, as did their secular equivalents: 'my generals, my prefects, my bishops'.

The Restoration brought back the 83 bishoprics. After the era of Revolution and war, the cathedral was carried along on a new symbolic wave, becoming one of the great Romantic myths. Chateaubriand was its bard, in particular resuscitating in the structure of cathedrals, not stone, but primitive wood, which conferred upon the cathedral its sacred origin, the forests of Gaul. The Romantic metaphor of the cathedral as forest would henceforth persist, as Baudelaire would exclaim: 'Great woods, you frighten me as do cathedrals.'

The great resurrection of cathedrals culminated in the response to Victor Hugo's novel *Notre-Dame de Paris* (known in English as *The Hunchback of Notre Dame*). In the wake of Romanticism, the end of the nineteenth century, especially in France, saw the myth of the cathedral flourishing, with Paul Verlaine exalting:

Led by the unique folly the Cross has brought,
O mad Cathedral, soaring on stony wings![5]

Joris-Karl Huysmans built a symbolist cathedral in his work *La Cathédrale* (1898), inspired by John Ruskin. Following John Constable and Caspar David Friedrich, who had painted Romantic cathedrals, Monet painted his Impressionist cathedrals, portraying aspects of Rouen Cathedral under the myriad lights and colours he experienced throughout the day. Claude Debussy evoked *La Cathédrale engloutie* (*The Submerged Cathedral*) in the first book of his piano preludes.

Two other important currents in the nineteenth century, however, complemented the status of cathedrals. In Germany, Romanticism ushered in increasingly close connections between Germanic tradition, political power and the Gothic art of cathedrals. The greatest expression of this is seen in the completion of Cologne Cathedral from 1824 to 1880, when it was solemnly inaugurated by Kaiser Wilhelm II. The other essential current was seen in the new-found passion for history and the efforts that were made to resurrect the past integrally, in what Jules Michelet called the 'scientific' resurrection of cathedrals. The embodiment of this mindset and its practice is found in the restoration of Notre-Dame de Paris, which had been anticipated earlier by the architect Ludovic Vitet who, when discussing Gothic cathedrals in his *Monographie de l'église Notre-Dame de Noyon* (1847), insists on 'the relationships that connected the origins and progress of new architecture to the social revolution of the twelfth century'. The great restorer of Notre-Dame de Paris, Eugène-Emmanuel Viollet-le-Duc, echoes this concept when he writes in his *Dictionnaire raisonné de l'architecture française* (1854–68): 'At the end of the twelfth century, building a cathedral was a need, because it was a dazzling protest against feudalism . . . The cathedrals of the twelfth and thirteenth centuries are in my view symbols of French nationalism and the most powerful attempts at unity.'

The cathedral was a great monument for the nineteenth century, which was enthralled by history, impassioned by nationalism, and roiled with a democratic spirit. The conflicts surrounding secularism at the end of the nineteenth century and the early twentieth are also found in the attitudes of great writers and artists of the time *vis-à-vis* cathedrals. If the great sculptor Auguste Rodin, in his book *Les Cathédrales de France* (1914) says 'The cathedral is the synthesis of the country, all of France is in its cathedrals', and therefore considers them eternal, Marcel Proust, 'in search of lost time', saw cathedrals as being lost there, as expressed in 'La mort des cathédrales', his desperate piece in *Le Figaro* (16 August 1904),

The twentieth century, far from allowing them to fade away, might be defined as a period of the resurrection of cathedrals. A balance was established between the cathedral as a place of worship for the faithful, and the cathedral as a place of spiritual emotion for visiting tourists. A great theatrical success testifies to the permanence of the cathedral as a mythical, exceptional place. In 1170 the Archbishop of Canterbury, Thomas Becket, was murdered in his cathedral, upon the orders of King Henry II of England. In 1935 the great English poet of American origin T. S. Eliot made the story the subject of his verse drama *Murder in the Cathedral*, which was first performed in the Chapter House of Canterbury, close to where the actual event happened.

The Second Vatican Council (1959) gave a balanced definition of the cathedral. In the end, the cathedral has been further enriched with new status and new meanings. According to Pierre Nora, as echoed by André Vauchez, it has become a 'lieu de mémoire', a place of memory. And, since it represents a connection between seeing and believing, according to Roland Recht it is a 'visual system'. The cathedral remains an enchanted and enchanting place.

Two images of Charlemagne. Top: Charlemagne the king of France sends his messengers out to all the empire. Bottom: Charlemagne is crowned by Pope Leo II at St Peter's in Rome. Miniature from a French manuscript of 1450.

CHARLEMAGNE

Charlemagne was a historical figure, a great witness to medieval history and its imaginary, who became increasingly mythical in his own lifetime.

The characteristics of the man (742–814) and the events of his reign (768–814) that helped to develop Charlemagne's image into that of a mythical hero were his accession to power, his wars and conquests, his imperial coronation, the importance for his entire empire of the institutions he founded and the texts he inspired, and the impact of the cultural measures that have remained throughout history and are known as the 'Carolingian Renaissance'.

His father, Pepin the Short (r. 751–68), was elected by an assembly of the Franks, making him the ruler of a new Frankish dynasty. To secure the legitimacy of the dynasty, Pepin, Charlemagne and his younger brother, Carloman, who died suddenly in 771, were anointed and crowned twice, first by the Franks, and again in 754 by Pope Stephen II.

Charlemagne was foremost a warrior, as were most of the heroes of the Middle Ages; the people of his time were astonished by the scale of his military campaigns and his conquests. His principal campaigns were against the Germanic peoples, the Saxons, whom he fought ferociously, although even the most admiring of his contemporaries were shocked by the number of prisoners who were executed. Farther east, he defeated the Bavarians and the Avars, while his victory against the Lombards in Italy led him to play the role of protector of the papacy. He established buffer zones on the borders of this great kingdom, non-linear boundaries called *Marks* in the Germanic language and *marches* in Frankish. The main *marches* were set up opposite the Scandinavians, the Slavs, the Bretons and the peoples of northern Spain. Charlemagne, for the first time in the West since the end of the fifth century, was crowned emperor in Rome by Pope Leo III on Christmas Day 800, in St Peter's Basilica and not in the cathedral church of the diocese of Rome, the Archbasilica of St John Lateran. This event created a situation that muddied the waters of Charlemagne's image throughout the Middle Ages. Like Arthur, Charlemagne was basically a king, the king of the Franks in fact, but his imperial title, accompanied by the special coronation ritual in Rome, made him a figure apart, who attempted to assert his superiority over other Christian kings through his status reflecting a return to antiquity and to the Roman Empire. This ambiguity between his royal and his imperial status was both his strength and his weakness. Although it allowed Charlemagne, and to a lesser extent other emperors of the Middle Ages, to assert himself above other kings, it distanced him from the royal status that was the most specific and the highest form of political power in the Middle Ages. The interplay between the royal and imperial functions was also one of the main reasons for the ephemeral nature of the Carolingian political construct. Europe was evolving toward the creation of nations, not remaining within the functioning of an empire. Under the aegis of Charlemagne, the emperors had to create a bastard political entity, the Germanic Holy Roman Empire, asserting both the importance of the Germanic character and the prestige of the Roman coronation.

Until recently the myth of Charlemagne has persisted mainly inside the nations that were heirs to his empire. The Charlemagne of his contemporaries began to assume a mythical allure in three domains: that of space, given the unheard-of expansion of his empire; that of institutions, in particular through the introduction of laws, the capitulars, which were implemented throughout the empire by travelling representatives of the sovereign, the *missi dominici*; and in the realm of culture with the creation of schools for future monks and sons of the aristocracy, which much later was to assume truly mythical importance.

Only after his death, not far into the ninth century, would Charlemagne be given the name 'grand' – *magnus* – which, when attached to 'Charles', confirmed his status as Charlemagne. It was in this period between history and myth that the first *Life of Charlemagne* appeared, written before 840 by Einhard, a Frankish aristocrat who had known Charlemagne well, especially in his final years. Einhard tends to paint a realistic portrait of his figure, but he sometimes alters it, first in the manner of the literary work he is imitating, Suetonius' *De vita Caesarum* (AD 121), and then to voice the Frankish patriotism the two men shared. Faithful to his ancient model, Einhard provides a physical portrait of Charlemagne that was carried into his mythical image. Charlemagne was impressive, and would be increasingly so, first in his physique. The emperor was stately, stood almost two metres tall, 'the top of his head was round; his eyes were very large and piercing. His nose was rather larger than is usual; he had beautiful white hair; and his expression was brisk and cheerful.' But, according to Einhard, 'Although his neck was rather thick and short and he was somewhat corpulent, this was not noticed owing to the good proportions of the rest of his body . . . his voice was clear, but hardly so strong as you would have expected.'¹ Such a portrait could only leave the impression of a colossus, which would later be confirmed by the exhumations of his corpse.

As seen in the excellent analysis by Claudio Leonardi, Einhard's *Life* makes it possible to understand that from the beginning, although Charles's identity was Germanic, and although he sought to appropriate Roman traditions, it remained true, according to the Italian historian Gustavo Vinay, that 'the king was Frankish from head to toe'.

Like all heroes, especially those of the Middle Ages, Charlemagne was closely associated with certain places, in particular with his tomb; cults of the main heroes of the Middle Ages, the saints and kings, in general developed around and out of their tombs. One of the first places associated with Charlemagne was Rome, the site of his coronation in 800. Then, especially after this itinerant king sought to settle down in a potential capital after several stays in conquered Saxony, notably in Paderborn, there was Aachen (Aix-la-Chapelle), where he ultimately chose to reside.

The palace complex at Aachen was the most important site linked to the living Charlemagne, destined to display and promote his image and serve his myth long after his death. The large audience hall and the huge octagonal chapel are located at either end of two long galleries, joined by a gate-house, that bring together the dual functions of the royal and imperial palace: family residence and government seat. Aachen was the only capital of a medieval hero, but soon its role was rapidly collapsing. It was no longer the main imperial seat and it served only for the coronation of new emperors as German kings, and even that stopped in the early sixteenth century.

After the coronations of Charles v in 1520 and Ferdinand I in 1530, Aachen was replaced in this function by Frankfurt-am-Main.

The events around Charlemagne's tomb have been splendidly described by Olaf B. Rader. There was a great fascination with Charlemagne's body, which was believed to confer power on the one who exhumed it, and so the tomb was opened on a number of occasions, perhaps starting in the year 1000, certainly in 1165, and several times down to the twentieth century, the last one in 1998. The exhumation of the year 1000, done at the behest of Emperor Otto III, who was eager to solemnly receive Charlemagne's patronage for the Ottonian dynasty, certainly did not occur as told by the *Chronicle of Novalese* around 1030:

> So we approached Charles. He was not lying down, as is the custom for bodies of other dead people, but was sitting on a sort of throne as though alive. He was crowned with a golden crown, holding a scepter in his hands, which were clothed in gloves, through which his actual fingernails had protruded. Over him, there was a small building made of rock and marble, well fashioned. When we got to it, immediately we made a hole in it by breaking it. But when we entered it, we perceived a very strong fragrance. We therefore immediately worshipped him on bent knees; and straightaway the Emperor Otto dressed him in white vestments, and cut his nails, and repaired everything in disrepair around him. In truth there was nothing lacking from his limbs through putrefaction, but at the tip of his nose there was a small piece missing. Otto restored it immediately with gold and, taking one tooth from Charles's mouth, took his leave after the building had been reconstructed.[2]

Although it is possible that the tomb was indeed opened, which does correspond to the mythical tastes of Otto III and to the sensibilities of the year 1000, it is certain that Charlemagne's corpse was not found sitting up in his tomb.[3] Such a rite would not have been accepted by the Church, and the fiction served only to highlight the importance of royal objects, the regalia of royal heroes. In addition to the sword – Charlemagne's was called Joyeuse – there was the crown and, in this case, the throne. But, even if Charlemagne's corpse was meant to enhance the status of the hero's image, death, the remains, were above all proof of the mortality even of heroes. The lesson of Charlemagne's exhumation was to show proof through the mortal remains that a royal hero, just like other men, must wait for the signal of the resurrection at the end of time.

Furthermore, as we saw with Arthur, Charlemagne exhibited another characteristic of royal heroes: their weakness – they were not saints. Very soon after his death, there was talk of the sin of Charlemagne. With the help of the Church, Charlemagne was able to hide his repudiation of several of his wives, which shows that the Frankish king had remained polygamous. The lavish affection that the emperor bestowed upon his daughters led very early on to suspicions of incest and, as we have seen, such suspicion was easily attributed to royal heroes; but Charlemagne's sin was incest with his sister, and the fruit of that incest was Roland. So, the medieval tendency to surround royal heroes with members of their families and knights of great merit is also found with Charlemagne. In this mythical grouping we find alongside Charlemagne his nephew Roland, various peers and *preux*; the chivalrous hero in the Middle Ages alternated between solitude and a structured entourage: his family and court.

The exhumation ordered in Aachen by Frederick I Barbarossa in 1165 had repercussions that repay attention. Here is how it is presented in a charter by the emperor dated 8 January 1166:

> Therefore, boldly inspired by the glorious deeds and merits of the most holy emperor Charles; by the zealous petition of our dearest friend Henry, illustrious king of England; by the persuasive assent and authority of our lord Pope Pascal; and with the counsel of all our princes, both secular and ecclesiastical, we gathered at our annual Christmas court at Aachen for the revelation, exaltation, and canonization of his [Charlemagne's] most holy body. There, at Aachen, his most holy body had been securely buried for fear of hostile foreigners and domestic enemies, but it was made manifest by divine revelation for the praise and glory of the name of Christ, for the strengthening of the Roman Empire, and for the well-being of our beloved consort, the Empress Beatrice, and our sons, Frederick and Henry. We raised up and exalted that body with great fear and reverence on December 29th in the presence of a great assembly of princes and a copious multitude of clerics and people singing hymns and sacred canticles.[4]

The event that marked the history of the myth of Charlemagne during the 1165 ceremonies at Aachen was the emperor's fragile accession to the status of saint. In the text just cited, Frederick Barbarossa explains the context of that decision. His reference to the king of England, Henry II, is related to Henry's attempts to have the Anglo-Saxon king Edward the Confessor canonized by Pope Alexander III. He mentions Pascal II, as he was the pope who should normally have had the authority to canonize Charlemagne. Not only did Frederick Barbarossa want to assert his own power in regard to canonizations, but he knew that Pascal II had been elected pope thanks to his intervention and did not have sufficient status to make saints canonically. That was, moreover, the outcome. Pascal II remained an anti-pope, and when the Church increasingly reserved the official right to canonize for the papacy, it did not acknowledge the sainthood of Charlemagne. Curiously, that sainthood survived in the folkloric margins of the myth of Charlemagne, since, as we will see, in the late nineteenth century the emperor became the patron of schoolchildren, and St Charlemagne's Day was celebrated in schools, including secular schools. In France, in particular, there was a celebration for the winners of an open competition that was held on 28 January, a date outside the canonical calendar that had unofficially become St Charlemagne's Day.

The myth of Charlemagne continued to develop throughout the Middle Ages, primarily in France and Germany, but also in Italy, the three major realms of the historical Carolingian empire. As national sentiments began to develop, so did a duel between the Germans and the French concerning Charlemagne's patronage. But the myth of Charlemagne went beyond the central realm of Christendom. Its appearance among Slavs can be seen in those languages in which the name Charles became the generic term for 'king', Russian and Polish in particular (*kral, korol, král, krol*), which indicates that Charlemagne was viewed more as a king than an emperor.

A curious extension of the myth of Charlemagne was its connection to the world of the Crusades. From the end of the eleventh century until the thirteenth Charlemagne was one of the spearheads, one of the guarantors of the adventure of the Christian Crusades. The influence of popular literary works, such as the *Chanson de Roland* and *Le Pèlerinage de Charlemagne à Jérusalem et à Constantinople* (Charlemagne's Pilgrimage to Jerusalem and Constantinople), certainly played a major role in this regard. Charlemagne was the hero of a mythical Christendom, emerging from a strictly Christian space: in Spain, in the Byzantine world and in Muslim Palestine.

The myth of Charlemagne even penetrated the Scandinavian world. At an uncertain time between the twelfth and thirteenth centuries a Norse saga starring Charlemagne was written, presumably commissioned by King Haakon IV Haakonarson, King of Norway (r. 1217–63). The *Karlamagnús saga* includes ten chapters or 'branches', the first of which traces the life of Charlemagne; the third connects to this the story of the hero Ogier the Dane; the seventh tells of Charlemagne's journey to Jerusalem and Constantinople; the eighth is dedicated to the battle of Roncesvalles; and the tenth and last assembles miracles and various signs around Charlemagne and his death.

By now, however, Charlemagne's physical appearance had changed. Einhard's hero, though mainly described in his later years, was clean-shaven and vigorous. At a date that cannot be determined, Charlemagne became 'the emperor with the flowing beard'. The white hair in Einhard's portrait, no doubt following the whims of fashion – we would probably find a comparable evolution in the face of Christ – must have led to the appearance of a white beard. It adorns Charlemagne's chin in the *Chanson de Roland*, in which the emperor, sad and discouraged, often cries, tugging on his white beard. In Germany, though the image of the mythical emperor reached its apogee with the majestic portrait that Dürer painted in 1512 for the Treasure Chamber in the Schopper House in Nuremberg, offering the definitive image of the emperor with the flowing beard, the myth of Charlemagne, after fading for a time, resumed an important role within Romanticism and through Prussian political undertakings in the nineteenth century.

But it is certainly in France that we can, along with the historian Robert Morrissey, best follow the evolution of the myth of the emperor with the flowing beard. In the twelfth century Charlemagne appeared in the *Historia Karoli Magni*, or *Pseudo-Turpin Chronicle*, and the Capetian dynasty attempted to associate itself with the mythical king-emperor. This was the *redditus ad stirpem Karoli*, a return to Charles's lineage sought by Philippe Auguste (r. 1180–1223). On the one hand, the king wed Isabella of Hainault, daughter of Baldwin V, Count of Flanders, availing himself of Carolingian blood, and on the other hand, Gilles de Paris, canon of Saint-Marcel, introduced Charlemagne as a model to Philippe Auguste's young son, the future Louis VIII, in the *Carolinus*, a long instructional poem written in 1195–6.

From the fifteenth century to the twentieth Charlemagne faded from time to time, but he never disappeared and his myth was resurrected forcefully in various periods. In the fifteenth century, the poet François Villon proved Charlemagne's persistence in the French imaginary: the refrain of his ballad *Seigneurs du temps jadis* ('Lords of Bygone Days') is 'But where is the *preux* Charlemagne?' The fashionable court of Philip the Good, Duke of Burgundy (r. 1419–67), was enthralled with the *Chroniques et conquestes de Charlemagne* compiled by David Aubert. A very intense moment in the cult of Charlemagne occurred during the reign of Charles VIII (r. 1483–98), who presented himself as a new Charlemagne and placed his Italian campaigns under the patronage of the great Charles. Humanist history presented a nuanced Charlemagne whereas, increasingly, and culminating in the Revolution, the historical heroes offered to the French were heroes from antiquity and more specifically from

REPUBLIQUE FRANÇAISE

0,60 CHARLEMAGNE _POSTES

French stamp with an illustration of the emperor Charlemagne in the popular imagination, bearded and crowned, 1966.

Roman antiquity. Étienne Pasquier, in his *Recherches de la France* (1560), desacralized Charlemagne. The classical era strove unconvincingly to revive an absolutist Charlemagne, one who would announce the Sun King. Voltaire saw Charlemagne as an anti-hero, and in the mythology of the kings of France replaced him with Henri IV.

One of the great revivals of the myth of Charlemagne obviously occurred in the Napoleonic era. Napoleon was personally committed to it, made the journey to Aachen, and planned his coronation to follow that of Charlemagne by forcing the pope's participation, but decreasing the pontiff's role even further by holding the ceremony in Notre-Dame de Paris, rather than in Rome. The emperor of the French also placed on his own head the crown that had probably been placed on Charlemagne by Leo III. Romantic enthusiasm took hold of Charlemagne, and Victor Hugo in *Hernani* (1830), employing the symbolism of the tomb found in the mythology of heroes, has the future Charles V kneel in front of the tomb of Charlemagne:

Charlemagne! It is you!
Oh! Since God, for whom all obstacles are erased,
Take our two majesties and put them face to face,
Pour me in the heart, from the bottom of this tomb,
Something great, sublime and beautiful!
Oh! From every side make me see everything.
Show me that the world is small because I do not dare touch it…
Teach me your secrets of conquering and reigning
And tell me that it is better to punish than to forgive!
Is it not? …
Oh! Tell me what can be done after Charlemagne!

From the second half of the nineteenth century the myth of Charlemagne faded away, except in one realm in which it assumed astonishing importance: though Charlemagne was no longer the patron saint of schoolchildren, he became their secular patron. He visited schools and was an attentive inspector of national education. Finally, after the Second World War Charlemagne was reborn with the construction of Europe. While historians passionately debate whether or not he was the first great European, Charlemagne, who was not really of much interest to the worlds of film and television,[5] became the symbol of Franco-German reconciliation and the patron of Europe. The post-war municipality of Aachen created a Charlemagne Prize, which has been awarded to the greats of European construction, from Jean Monnet to Adenauer and Robert Schuman, to those great Europeans who came from behind the Iron Curtain, such as the Czech writer Václav Havel and the Polish historian Bronisław Geremek, and even to great Americans, such as Bill Clinton, as protectors of Europe. Charlemagne is a good example of the ebb and flow of mythicized historical heroes and of the continuity of the history of the imaginary.

EL CID

El Cid is an example of a historical medieval figure who passed from the realm of history into the world of mythology.

This medieval figure is unique for having travelled through time to the present day with his image unchanged. Rodrigo Díaz de Vivar, known as El Cid (1043–1099), is an exemplary figure of the Spanish Christian *Reconquista* over the Moors. In the twelfth century, through a literary *oeuvre* sustained and expanded in legends and oral storytelling, he became a Christian hero in the battle against the Moors, and ultimately, through seventeenth-century dramatic adaptations, the hero of a great love story that would continue to be told on stage and screen, and even in opera.

Rodrigo Díaz, born in Vivar, a small town in Castile near Burgos, was a knight of the minor nobility who put his talents as a fighter and nobleman at the service of either the kings of Castile or of Muslim emirs. After serving Alfonso VI, king of Léon and Castile, in his fight against the Christian king of Navarre, he was exiled by Alfonso in 1081 and put his sword to use alongside the Moorish king of Saragossa in his battle against the count of Barcelona and the king of Aragon and Navarre; this was when he was given the nickname 'El Cid', from the Arabic *al-sayyid*, meaning 'lord'. Later reconciled with Alfonso VI, he was victorious in defending the

Christians against an invading force of North African Almoravids in eastern Spain, where he established a principality for himself. At first in the service of a Muslim prince allied with Alfonso, he freed himself from that relationship and in 1094 seized Valencia, where he installed the first Christian state on Islamic land. He demanded the payment of tributes from small neighbouring Islamic Taïfa kingdoms. In 1102, however, three years after his death, his widow Jimena and Alfonso VI were forced to abandon the Valencia principality to the Moors. Denis Menjot has described the historical El Cid well: 'He was a "border adventurer", avid for chivalric exploits and spoils, serving Christian and Muslim rulers whose wars ensured his social promotion, consecrated by the marriage of his daughters with the king of Navarre and the count of Barcelona.'

In the twelfth century this historical figure was transformed into a Christian hero fighting Muslims, an emblematic figure of the Spanish *Reconquista*. This transformation was due primarily to the notoriety bestowed upon Díaz de Vivar and his wife Jimena by the monks of the Benedictine monastery of San Pedro de Cardeña, near Burgos, where the couple were buried. El Cid was not only a Christian hero, but a Castilian hero, even though the great adventure of his career was the establishment of the principality near Valencia. But it was a literary text that definitively ensured El Cid's reputation beyond the borders of Castile. It is a poem, a *chanson de geste*, written in Castilian between 1110 and 1150 by an anonymous poet, titled *Cantar de mío Cid* (also later known as the *Poema de mío Cid*). The El Cid of the *cantar* is Castilian, serves only Christians and fights Muslims. The *Cantar* tells of a series of sieges, raids and battles in which El Cid is always a Christian commander. Another theme in the poem is the difficult relations between El Cid and his liege lord, the king of Castile, illustrating the issues of the feudal hierarchy.

Finally, the El Cid of the *Cantar*, in addition to carrying out heroic deeds as a fighter, is concerned with ensuring the glory and future of his family lineage through his two daughters, despite their matrimonial disappointments. His daughters married two *infantes* from another great noble Castilian family, the *infantes* of Carrion, but their insulting behaviour towards their father-in-law, and their generally scandalous behaviour, ended in a legal duel and their defeat. El Cid and Jimena's daughters, as is known, eventually had good marriages; in this realm, too, El Cid was victorious.

Shortly before his death in 1099, Rodrigo Díaz was celebrated in a Latin poem, the *Carmen Campidoctoris*, an ode to the noble warrior that earned him his other nickname, El Campeador. The renown of the Castilian hero was ensured by a mid-thirteenth-century chronicle that was also devoted to him, the *Historia Roderici*.

The monks of Cardeña took advantage of his elevated reputation and made an unsuccessful attempt to have El Cid canonized. Although his canonization was not officially recognized, the reputation of this quasi-saint continued to grow when Alfonso x the Wise made a pilgrimage to Cardeña in 1272. The monks had El Cid's tomb opened in 1541 and noted the odour of sainthood that escaped from it. In 1554 Philip ii of Spain received permission from the Vatican to initiate canonization procedures, but these were soon abandoned.

Nonetheless the hero's fame continued to grow, at least in Castile. A chronicle, probably written at the beginning of the fourteenth century, was printed in Burgos in 1512 under the title *Crónica del famoso cavallero Cid Ruy Díez Campeador*, and was reprinted in 1552 and 1593.

But it was the theatre that would relaunch the transformed mythical image of El Cid. Although the historical, chivalric Rodrigo is certainly emphasized in plays, a different side of his character also

Rodrigo Diaz
de Vivar,
El Cid.

RODERIC
DE VIVAR

appears, that of the great lover. The love between Rodrigo and Jimena
finds itself thwarted, thereby offering a dramatic theme in Spanish
theatre at the end of the Golden Age. Classical French theatre, which
adopted the Hispanicist tradition, found an exemplary figure in the
hero caught between passion and duty. In 1561, using mainly popular ballads in which the love theme had flourished, the Spanish
playwright Guillén de Castro had staged *Las Mocedades de Rodrigo*
(The Youthful Deeds of Rodrigo), which inspired Corneille's *Le
Cid*, whose first performance in Paris in 1636 was a huge success;
Corneille's play would later be the source for Jules Massenet's opera
Le Cid (1885).

El Cid seems to have escaped the Romantic period. His literary
image was probably too connected to that of a masterpiece of
classical theatre. The historical figure, however, was undermined,

if not almost destroyed, by a Dutch scholar of Arabic, Reinhart Dozy, who, in his *Recherches sur l'histoire politique et littéraire de l'Espagne pendant le Moyen Age* (1849), introduced the man whom he called 'the Cid according to new documents'. One of his main sources was the Arab scholar Ibn Bassam (d. 1147) from Santarem, Portugal, who, while in Seville, wrote his *Treasury of the Virtues of the People of the Peninsula*, a biographical dictionary in which he drew an unflattering portrait of El Cid Campéador. Dozy re-established the historical image of a cruel and crude *condottiere* in the place of the pious and courtly knight of the Spanish legend. He even declared that El Cid had been more Muslim than Christian.

But at the beginning of the twentieth century there was a revival of El Cid, the Spanish hero, thanks to *La España del Cid* (1929), a masterpiece by the illustrious philologist and literary historian Ramón Menéndez Pidal. Showing considerable erudition and unparalleled literary talent, Menéndez Pidal turned El Cid into the eponymous and central hero of a glorified medieval Spain. Thanks to Menéndez Pidal, El Cid had finally attained the zenith of his national glory, and in a certain sense he represented the Spanish figure of the hero within the heroic landscape of Europe. Francoism attempted to appropriate El Cid, even making connections between El Cid and Caudillo, the title taken by Francisco Franco. Menéndez Pidal would not accept such deformations, and for a few years he was stripped of the presidency of the Spanish Academy by the regime. But he was not really a true opponent of the regime, including on this issue.

Although El Cid, in spite of the many criticisms made against Menéndez Pidal's study, remains an exemplary hero of the Middle Ages, of a Middle Ages gripped by nationalism, in the second half of the twentieth century he experienced a new, glorious avatar thanks,

Gérard Philipe playing Corneille's El Cid at a production staged in the
Palace of the Popes, Avignon, 1951.

once again, to the theatre. The conjunction between resolutely
modern productions and the promotion of charismatic actors who
played Rodrigo's character as a young, chivalric hero turned Corneille's
play into a great success for the director Jean Vilar at the Théâtre
National Populaire, Paris, and the Avignon Festival in 1949–51.
Although the very traditionalist actor Mounet-Sully had played a
quite 'classical' Cid at the Comédie Française in 1885 (the same year,

incidentally, as Jules Massenet's opera *Le Cid*, based on Corneille), in Vilar's production a young El Cid was revealed by Gérard Philipe, then just 27 years old, who enthralled his audiences. Other directors and actors have also shown that El Cid could be a hero in the most modern of theatre experiences. El Cid is therefore an example of a historical hero promoted by literature and theatre, thereby bringing together the various agents who produce the heroic imaginary: memory, poetry, theatre and, of course, human beings.

Without enjoying the same success in cinema, El Cid inspired at least one famous film, that directed by Anthony Mann (1961) and starring Charlton Heston and Sophia Loren. More recently, a film has shown that El Cid, like King Arthur, is one of those historical heroes whom contemporary history can readily manipulate. In the Spanish animated film *El Cid: La leyenda* (dir. José Pozo, 2003), for example, El Cid is a fearless fighter, beyond reproach, a great slayer of Moors who are bloodthirsty, devoid of any moral sense and led by a bearded and cruel chieftain.

THE CLOISTER

The word 'cloister' has persisted in the European imaginary up to the present time and highlights two characteristic components of monastic ideology. The cloister in the historical imaginary is primarily a central place in a monastery, made up of an inner garden surrounded by galleries that open onto the garden through arcades. The cloister can also refer to the entire monastery as a grouping of enclosed buildings. The essential meaning of the term in both cases is the notion of closing off, of enclosure. It comes from the Latin word *claustrum*, which is associated with *claudere*, to shut.

The cloister, then, reflects an image of enclosure, linked in the Christian imaginary to that of the garden. The medieval garden par excellence was enclosed, and that enclosure protected both the monks' vegetable and fruit harvests and the spiritual space with which, beginning in the eleventh and twelfth centuries, the image of the Virgin would be principally associated. When the Virgin escaped the trials of her earthly life, she went either to heaven, after the Assumption, or into an enclosed garden. The cloister as an enclosed garden essentially refers to paradise, and medieval symbolic thinking did in fact often speak of the monastic cloister as a paradise.

The walled garden and the fountain at its centre, from *Speculum humanae salvationis*, 15th century.

Beyond the image of celestial Jerusalem, the cloister was also a metaphor for the heart and for one's inner self; it was the part of Christian ideology that became a symbol of inner peace in the face of the agitations of the world, in complementary contrast to the peregrinations of *homo viator*, itinerant man.

The cloister was thus the embodiment of one side of ambivalent medieval Christianity and of the European sensibility that emerged from it. If, indeed, while looking at knights we have seen that medieval man's fundamental relationship with space primarily involved wandering, the other antithetical yet complementary side of medieval Christianity was a connection to a specific place, to what monastic language called *stabilitas loci* (stability of place). Thus, the men – and, to a lesser degree, the women – of the medieval West oscillated between a place of attachment and the open road.

The cloister appeared in western monastic architecture as early as the fourth century. A document from about 820 in the Carolingian period indicates that the cloister held a central place in both the structure and functioning of the Christian monastery. The document is a plan of St Gall Abbey, in present-day Switzerland. It is both a reflection of the real monastery and a representation of the monastic ideal. The cloister, in the wider sense of monastery, appears in it as a sort of self-sufficient city. Its centre is very clearly the church and the cloister attached to it. The expansion of a monastery and its annexes into a true city has been verified for the Carolingian period by Saint-Riquier Abbey in Picardy.

The great surge in monastic cloisters dates from the Romanesque period (eleventh–twelfth centuries). Modern aesthetic tastes view the Romanesque cloisters that have been preserved, for example in Provence, as among the most beautiful bequeathed by medieval architecture, whereas, as we have seen, the cathedral par excellence is Gothic in style. In this stylistic opposition we find the contrast between the intimate and the open that characterized medieval ideology and sensibility. The cloister as a closed space inside a monastery was the place where the monks' communal spirit and the element of individual devotion conveyed by the word 'monk' (Greek *monos*, 'alone') were best embodied. The cloister was a place of individual prayer. It was the framework par excellence of that fundamental exercise of Christian devotion. But the galleries of the cloister could be the theatre of collective demonstrations of devotion, for example the processions of monks.

It appears that the cloister was at its apogee in monastic life during the reforms of the twelfth century, the most famous of which was that of the Cistercians. The glorification of the cloister was a major theme in the monastic spirituality and literature of the twelfth century. The two most remarkable accounts reflecting this are *De disciplina claustrali* (School of the Cloister) by the Benedictine Peter Cellensis (d. 1183) and *De claustro animae* (the Cloister of the Soul) by the Augustinian canon Hugh of Fouilloy (d. 1174). Peter Cellensis insists on the virtues of the cloister: the tranquillity of the soul (*quies*) and idleness used for devotion (*otium*). Hugh of Fouilloy gives an allegorical explanation of the different parts of the cloister. We can indeed see that the cloister was the symbolic expression of solitude and the contemplative life as opposed to the active life.

Monastic spirituality, especially among the Benedictines, turned to art and in particular to sculpture, both to pay homage to God and as a means to elevate the soul. The galleries of cloisters were often magnificently adorned with sculptures. Among the most beautifully decorated are the cloister of Moissac Abbey in southwestern France, dated by an inscription to 1100, and that of Saint-Trophime at Arles, in Provence.

The mendicant orders, who lived in cities in structures that were no longer called cloisters, rather convents, still kept the inner space of the cloister, which henceforth followed the evolution of aesthetic tastes from Gothic to Renaissance and Baroque. A good example of a Baroque cloister is the one designed by Francesco Borromini and built in 1636 next to the church of San Carlo alle Quattro Fontane in Rome.

Baroque cloister, constructed for the Borromini in the 17th century for San Carlo alle Quattro Fontane, Rome.

The principal role of the cloister had been one of closing up, of enclosure. That ideal and practice were imposed primarily on women (or were chosen by them). Beginning in the fifth century, nuns were subjected to a strict rule of enclosure. Even the sisters of the mendicant orders, including the Poor Clares, were cloistered, unlike the brothers, whose calling frequently led them outside the convent. The decretal *Periculoso* issued by Pope Boniface VIII in 1298 extended a vow of cloistering for all nuns. In the sixteenth century, whereas Protestant reform did away with monasteries, convents and cloistering, the Catholic Counter-Reformation extended and reinforced cloistering for women. A strict cloistering was one of the elements of the Carmelite reform led by Teresa of Ávila. Charles Borromeo, Archbishop of Milan, oversaw strict adherence to the cloistering of nuns. The Council of Trent decreed excommunication for any infraction of the vows of cloistering. In 1616 Francis de Sales and Jane Frances de Chantal were obliged, against their wishes, to accept that the new order they had founded, the Order of the Visitation of Holy Mary (the Visitandines), would be cloistered. The image of the cloister, following the vicissitudes of the French Revolution and the closing of many monasteries and convents, remained connected to the image of the nun. A duality was re-formed in the nineteenth century, contrasting charitable and active sisters, such as the Daughters of Charity of St Vincent de Paul, and cloistered nuns, whose emblematic image was that of the Carmelites. *Dialogues des Carmélites*, a 1952 play based on an unfilmed screenplay by Georges Bernanos, was turned into a powerful opera (1957) with libretto and music by Francis Poulenc that fixed this imaginary link between women and the cloister.

At the end of the nineteenth century and the beginning of the twentieth the cloister became a nostalgic image of a medieval monastic paradise. Representing the most perfect combination of architecture and sculpture, cloisters attracted the interest of rich collectors, and in particular American enthusiasts who considered them the highest expression of medieval art. Beginning in 1914, the sculptor George Grey Barnard assembled various fragments from medieval European abbeys. In 1925 John D. Rockefeller bought his collection and gifted it to the Metropolitan Museum of Art in New York. The following year the fragments were gathered together and exhibited to the public in an annex on a hill overlooking the Hudson River. Here can be seen the cloisters of Saint-Guilhem-le-Désert Abbey and Saint Michel de Cuxa, reconstructed almost in their entirety. Other sculptures, tapestries and architectural fragments surround these transferred and reconstituted cloisters. The ensemble was given the name 'The Cloisters'. Here the imaginary of the cloister is remembered and reincarnated in the emblematic city of contemporary America.

Most of the monasteries today are abandoned and their cloisters empty, but the cloister has become mythical through its evocation of solitude and paradise, while also offering an exceptional space for various musical performances. Noirlac Abbey in Berry is one of the most notable examples of those offering a wide range of attractions. Thus, in the European imaginary of today, the cloister has become the image of both a lost paradise and a destroyed or opened prison.

The jongleur of Bourges, 1175–1200, limestone.

THE JONGLEUR

The jongleur was an entertainer. His name comes from the Latin *jocus*, 'game', which explains his status and ambiguous image in medieval society and culture.

That ambiguity was also found in the notion of pleasure in that society and culture. The jongleur is the perfect example of the ambiguous hero. Edmond Faral saw the jongleur as the successor of ancient mimes. I am above all struck by his close connection to the new feudal society that was being put in place in the tenth to twelfth centuries. What is certain, however, is that he encompasses a portion of the legacy of pagan entertainers, in particular the Celtic bards. The jongleur was an itinerant entertainer who performed his *jongleries* wherever they would be enjoyed and remunerated, that is, essentially, in seigneurial castles. He was an all-around entertainer. He recited poetry and told stories. He was a jongleur 'of the mouth', but he was not the author of the texts he recited. They were written by troubadours and trouvères; he was only a performer.

At the same time, he was a jongleur of movement; an acrobat who performed contortions, a jongleur in the modern sense of the term, a dancer, often parodic. And finally, he was a musician who sang while often accompanying himself on the lute or the hurdy-gurdy. But everything depended on the content of the jongleur's performance and the meaning he gave to it. The jongleur was in some sense an illustration of man's dual nature: created by God, but fallen after original sin. His speech and actions could thus lean on either the good or the bad side, reveal his condition as a son of God created in his image, or as a sinner manipulated by the Devil. The jongleur could be the jongleur of God or the jongleur of Satan. He was the exemplary image of what every medieval hero fundamentally was: a heroic man, but a sinner in some way, one who might abandon his service to God and choose to serve Satan. One of the great tasks of medieval morality was to separate good from evil, the pure and the impure aspects of the behaviour of medieval heroes. This is seen in the questions asked about men's professions in the Middle Ages. Were they licit or illicit? And in the case of the jongleur, was the pleasure he provided, and which was the goal of his profession, licit or illicit?

A text from the beginning of the thirteenth century that has become famous among medievalists distinguishes between good and bad jongleurs. This text emerged from two social movements that took a strong look at the ambivalence of professions. One involved the burgeoning Scholastic method, a critical method for making distinctions, for ordering and classifying, which consequently sought to separate the true from the false, the licit from the illicit, and so on. The other movement, involving the development of aural confession, made obligatory by the Fourth Lateran Council of 1215, sought to define the moral and social benefits and dangers of each profession. From a confessor's manual dating to just before 1215, the Englishman Thomas of Chobham, trained at the University of Paris, distinguished between good and bad jongleurs. According to Thomas, the bad jongleur, the shameful (*turpis*) jongleur, was the one who did not recoil before *scurrilitas*, that is, buffoonery, excess, the exhibitionism of speech and gestures. He was the one who did not place his body in the service of the mind; he was a minstrel who replaced a decent gesture with an immodest *gesticulatio*. There were others, however, who were to be praised. They

> sing the praises of the great deeds of princes and the lives of the saints, they provide comfort when one is ill, or upset, and they do not commit too many infamies as do the men and women acrobats, as well as those who perform shameful spectacles and make ghosts appear either through incantations, or otherwise.

Licit or illicit, the medieval jongleur in all cases remained close to the limits of what medieval morality, the Church and feudal society allowed. He illustrated the fragile position of the heroes of the Middle Ages. More than others, he had a tendency to be marginal, and it is not by chance that we indeed often find him represented in the illustrated margins of manuscripts. There is, however, an illustrious jongleur in the Bible: David. King David was a king who played, sang and danced. Granted, he, too, had his weaknesses, in particular regarding Bathsheba, by whose charms he was drawn and with whom he committed adultery; but he remained a glorious model who supported the image of the jongleur when the Church or society was tempted to scorn or reject him.

According to Michel Zink, it was St Bernard of Clairvaux (d. 1153) who best rehabilitated the jongleur in twelfth-century feudal society. For St Bernard, jongleurs offered people an example of humility. And, having become humble, people resembled

> jongleurs and acrobats who, heads down and feet up, do the opposite of what is usual for people, they walk on their hands

and thereby draw the attention of everyone to them. It is not
a childish game, it is not a theatrical game that provokes desire
through shameful female undulations and which represent
ignoble acts, but an agreeable game, decent, serious, remarkable,
the viewing of which can rejoice celestial spectators.

The Church and Christians were divided at that point in the
twelfth century between the rehabilitation of jongleurs, as justified
by St Bernard, and their condemnation without appeal, as formu-
lated by Bernard's contemporary Honorius Augustodunensis in the
Elucidarium. A disciple asks the question: 'Do jongleurs have hope?'
and the master responds: 'Not the slightest, indeed, in everything
they mean to do they are servants of Satan; it is about them that
it is said: they haven't known God, that is why God will abandon
them when thieves will be mocked.' The opinion of the 'progressive'
Abelard was the same. He saw in jongleurs' activity a 'diabolical
preaching'. If the jongleur tended more and more to be not only
accepted but praised and admired, it was all the same only because
his image had changed since St Bernard, who in fact called himself a jongleur of God through humility. He indeed despised those
entertainers, and his attitude was akin to those exalted Christians
who became insane in order to humiliate themselves before God.

And so in the thirteenth century the jongleur became a truly
positive figure. He owed this in large part to the mendicant orders,
for example through St Francis of Assisi. No one in the Middle Ages
called themselves a 'jongleur of God' more strongly than he. All
the same, he specified that he was a jongleur 'of the mouth', that he
avoided gesticulations, but deemed that his preaching, through its
narrative and popular nature, was related to the salutary profession
of jongleurs.

Still in the thirteenth century, the Franciscan preacher Nicolas de Biard made the connection between confessors and jongleurs:

Jongleurs are confessors who elicit laughter and the joy of God and the saints through the excellence of their speech and their actions: the one reads in church, the other sings, one speaks in Roman, that is, that which is in Latin he says in the Romance language for the laypeople hearing his preaching.

It must be said that, from St Bernard to St Francis and Nicolas de Biard, a revolution had occurred in the manifestations of happiness and pleasure among Christians. Laughter, up to then mainly repressed as in the monasteries, was liberated. St Francis was a saint who knew how to laugh and who made laughter one of the expressions of his spirituality, that is, for those who saw and heard him, of his saintliness. Another Franciscan, Roger Bacon, proposed to 'establish preaching on a rhetoric of emotion, itself established on recourse to gestures, to mimicking, and even to the music and art of the jongleur'. The edifying romances of the Catalan Ramón Llull, at the end of the thirteenth century, portray worthy jongleurs. The jongleur was no longer only a diffuser of pleasure; he himself became a literary hero, primarily, it is true, when he was turned from a jongleur into a minstrel (or *menestrier*).

That change was connected both to a social evolution, and to the evolution of mentalities and culture. The itinerant jongleur now tended to earn a stable living, like the other professions that had settled in cities or castles; he became a stable, sedentary performer for a seigneurial patron. At the same time, the liberation of music and the spread of new musical instruments played by specialized musicians caused music to be more or less dropped from his repertoire. In Paris, a street called 'des Jongleurs', which indicates that it had become a recognized profession, at the end of the Middle Ages became the rue 'des Ménétriers'. Today it is rue Rambuteau.

A literary hero, the minstrel appeared, for example, in the romance *Cléomadès* by Adenes le Roi (around 1260).

A true minstrel must be careful
not to harm or defame;
no speech, however benign,
should come out of his mouth.
He must always be ready
To proclaim the good wherever it comes.
Blessed is he who acts this way!

Another minstrel, Colin Muset, who performed in Champagne and Lorraine in the mid-thirteenth century, sang of the instability of the jongleur's condition, as he sought to become a sedentary minstrel. He is addressing an ungenerous lord:

Lord count, I played
before you in your home,
and you didn't give me anything
or anything to make a living:
it's shameful!
By my faith in Saint Mary,
I will no longer follow you.
My alms container is empty,
And so is my purse.

Above all, there is an edifying tale that magnifies the figure of the jongleur by showing that he could interiorize his profession, his skills, without seeking an audience. This is the tale of the jongleur of Notre-Dame who, thinking he is alone, performs his show in front of a statue of the Virgin and Child to dedicate his talent and effort to them. If what he did was known and became a model of devotion, it is because a monk and the abbot of the monastery happened upon him during his solitary performance. *Le Jongleur de Notre-Dame* was for centuries a popular and inspiring work that would ensure a future for the heroic image of the jongleur. The culmination of this image is seen in the opera that Jules Massenet composed in 1902, under the influence of a revival of the music and sensibility of the Middle Ages, as expressed in the rebirth of Gregorian chant and inspired by the Schola Cantorum de Paris, a music conservatory founded in 1894.

But in the meantime, the image of the jongleur was profoundly changed. The phenomenon responsible for that change was the advent of a great social novelty in the world of entertainment: the birth of the circus in the second half of the sixteenth century. The jongleur was henceforth only one specialized artist among all the other circus artists. In it he represented the tricks and pleasures of nimbleness as opposed to those of danger. The acrobat became the trapeze artist, different from the jongleur, and the 'mouth' jongleur morphed into a completely new entertainer destined for a wonderful future in the modern world: the clown. That term appeared in English about 1560, then very quickly in French, in the forms of *cloyne, cloine* (1563), *clowne* (1567) and *cloune* (1570). In sixteenth-century England, the clown was a bumpkin who caused people to laugh in spite of themselves, a buffoon who found his place in Shakespeare's plays, once again the culmination and apogee of

CLÉMENCEAU
Le pas du commandité

Here, French prime minister Georges Clémenceau juggles with the consequences of his actions over the Panama Canal. *Le Petit Journal*, 19 August 1893.

medieval culture and sensibilities. But the clown is the heir of an image of the medieval hero, that of a man torn between laughter and tears.

Reduced to displaying his manual dexterity, the jongleur embraced other legacies that enriched his profession and his repertoire, one that came from as far away as China, and one that came out of the great success of the circus in nineteenth-century America. The jongleur did not completely recover his image despite the metaphorical use (halfway between admiration and condemnation) that was made of the wrongdoings of modern jongleurs: politicians and financiers. The jongleur exemplifies a marginal hero who was deconstructed and has blended into the modern and contemporary imaginary.

The first knights in combat, the Normans fighting the Saxons, in the Bayeux
Tapestry, end of the 11th century.

KNIGHTS AND CHIVALRY

Pierre Bonnassie has pointed out the difficulty of studying medieval chivalry:

> In the concept of chivalry, it is quite difficult to distinguish between myth and reality . . . It is the myth, that of the knight driven by absolutes and the avenger of the oppressed, which, through legend and literature – and ultimately cinema – has survived in the collective mind. In other words, the image of the medieval knight that we usually have today is nothing but an idealized image: it is precisely the image the chivalrous caste wanted to present of itself, and something it achieved and was able, with the help of trouvères, to impose on collective opinion.[1]

From the always illuminating point of view of vocabulary, the term *chevalier* (knight) appeared only in the Late Middle Ages, the initial term being *miles*, which in classical Latin means soldier, or in the High Middle Ages a free warrior. *Chevalier* is clearly related to *cheval* (horse) and the knight was foremost a man who had at least one horse and who fought on horseback. In the ideology of chivalry, the adjective *chevaleresque* (chivalrous) assumed great importance;

it should be noted that the Italian word *cavalleresco* appeared in the fourteenth century, and was translated into French only in the seventeenth century. The term, which today has a rather neutral, if not positive, connotation, then appeared in a fairly critical or even derisive context. This brings to mind Don Quixote. The knight's horse was obviously a special breed, sturdy, but capable of running fast when hunting or in battle, and was very different from the heavy draught horse that was gradually spreading throughout the medieval West. It was a charger.

The knight was above all a warrior, which in large part explains his status in a society in which war was omnipresent despite aspirations to peace, so we should take a moment to describe his fighting equipment. His main weapons were the long, double-edged sword, the spear with a shaft made of ash or beech wood, with a broad, sharp, iron head, and the wooden shield covered with leather, which could assume various shapes: round, oblong or almond-shaped. The rigid Roman breastplate gave way to a jerkin covered with metal pieces, or a leather tabard covered with metal scales arranged like slates on a roof. The helmet was in general only a simple iron dome, sometimes covered with leather. An important improvement came with the replacement of the jerkin with the hauberk, chainmail that covered the entire body from shoulders to knees, slit down the side to allow the knight to mount his horse, as can already be seen on the Bayeux Tapestry from the late eleventh century. Chainmail of this type, while very effective against blows from a sword, was insufficient against a spearhead wielded according to the new charging technique, one of the chief advancements in medieval military tactics.

As the historian Jean Flori has pointed out, the medieval knight needed massive financial resources to pay for his horse or horses and for his heavy equipment; he also needed time, because in addition to frequent training, the medieval knight had to prove himself in mock battles during festivals, known as tournaments, and in hunting, which was most often the exclusive prerogative of knights when they hunted outside royal deer parks, which in the Middle Ages were reserved for kings. All this meant that, from a military point of view, chivalry tended to be restricted to an aristocratic elite.

Chivalry developed in the eleventh century. The category of *milites* (and in the Latin vulgate, *caballarii*) became widespread around the year 1000, first in central and northern France, then in the Mediterranean regions and ultimately throughout Christendom. These *milites* were both fighters who served the higher nobility, and guardians of castles serving those same nobles; many of these castellans freed themselves from that role and became independent knights during the eleventh and twelfth centuries.

The appearance of *milites* occurred in a climate of suspicion maintained by the Church with regard to fighters, who were sometimes confused with bandits. This suspicion caused the *milites* to emerge within the context of a movement for peace, around the year 1000, which aimed to subdue the brutality of warriors and subject them to the directives of Christianity and the Church. And so the knights' mission was to protect widows and orphans, and more generally, the weak and the poor, including unarmed civilians, such as the first merchants.

During the eleventh century, however, the evolution that was distancing the Church and medieval Christianity from the pacifist spirit of early Christianity began to accelerate. When the Church started to embrace the idea that war was needed, indeed useful, under certain circumstances. The evolution became decisive when the Church embraced holy war, the Crusades, at the end of the eleventh century. Fighting for God and for the weak was sanctioned by new rituals, primarily dubbing, which was a sort of chivalric baptism. Dominique Barthélemy supports the idea of a convergence of chivalrous and Christian ideals as the foundation of feudalism.[2]

The Iberian peninsula was uniquely suited for the development of this Christian chivalry. The *Reconquista*, that is, the Christians' essentially military recapture of the peninsula from Muslims, brought knights to the forefront, and these *caballeros andantes españoles* became prestigious models not only for the Christians of the peninsula, but for all the inhabitants of Christendom.

The image of the knight was also superimposed on Christian kings, even if this second function did not overshadow the primary functions of wielder of justice and prosperity. The medieval king who is probably best remembered as also being a knight was Richard the Lionheart of England (r. 1189–99). Many historians have pointed out that Louis IX of France (St Louis) was never really seen as a knight, but in fact the image of the peacemaking king that he projected coexisted in his time with the image of the knight-king, which was seen both in his actions during the war against the English and, especially, during the Seventh and Eighth Crusades. The medieval chronicler Jean de Joinville has left an amazing image of St Louis, sword in hand, attempting to cross a dyke across the River Nile, with his horse's mane covered with Greek fire.

The Christianization of knights was also marked by persistent references to the saints who were their patrons and who held high-ranking places in medieval hagiography. In central and eastern Europe the black knight-saint St Maurice became the curious patron of white chivalry, but above all, throughout Christendom, the great chivalrous saint, also from the East, was St George. The religious and social role of this knight-saint was manifest in the most frequently depicted episode of his life, killing the dragon to save the princess. St George was the model of the courtly knight, using his strength, courage and saintly nature to serve the weak and powerless.

There was a difficult relationship, however, between the Church and knights that persisted throughout the Middle Ages, despite the Crusades and the emergence of a belief in just war. This can be seen in the history of the tournament. Tournaments, which were in a way the equivalent of contemporary major sporting events, enthralled both the chivalrous caste and the masses. They were associated both with military exercises and with entertainment, and in *Le dimanche de Bouvines* Georges Duby has shown how they were a very important and major economic enterprise. The Church, however, saw them as an out-of-control exaltation of violence, a transformation of just war into an exciting show, and felt that the profane, even pagan, aspects of these clashes were only too apparent. It therefore sought to ban tournaments. In particular, the Fourth Lateran Council in 1215 banished them from Christendom. But that move was a failure. Tournaments, condemned by the Church in 1139 and 1199, were allowed but controlled in England by Richard the Lionheart (1194), and after a certain lull continued into the thirteenth century. After the Church's ban was lifted in 1316, they even experienced an extraordinary surge in the fourteenth, fifteenth and sixteenth centuries. The developing monarchies were trying to monopolize tournaments by regulating them, and in particular by providing them with directors – heralds. The return of tournaments was a characteristic late flourish of the medieval world. One of the great entrepreneurs of tournaments during the flamboyant late Middle Ages was King René d'Anjou, Count of Provence and King of Naples, whose rules for the ordering of tournaments in his lands are laid out in a lavishly illuminated manuscript called *Traité de la forme et devis d'un tournois* (*c.* 1460).

Chivalry was the most characteristic expression of feudalism. As we have seen, it managed to combine quite easily its aristocratic nature, religious rituals and monarchical institutions. Georges Duby has shown how William Marshal (1147–1219), in his day considered 'the best knight in the world', owed his social success and status not only to his unwavering respect for the rules of chivalrous honour, but to the patronage of the king of England. Duby saw him as, if not the best, at least a typical knight, and describes him this way:

A younger son without prospects. Now rich and a baron, but as the guardian of his wife and her sons. Invested with royal authority, but as regent to the under-age king. Without imagining that he would ever accede to this degree of power. Without being trained to wield it, and without the title which might have come to him through blood or the priestly liturgy to do so. With no other virtue – and those who celebrated his virtues, speaking of him, repeating his own words, expressing what he, himself, believed, never sought to say anything different – than to be considered the flower of chivalry. It was to this excellence, and to it alone, that he owed his extraordinary elevation. To his great, indefatigable body, his strength and skill in knightly exercises; thanks to a brain that was apparently too small to hinder the natural bloom of his physical vigor with superfluous reasoning: few and brief thoughts, a stubborn attachment to the rough-hewn ethics of men of war whose values abide in three words: prowess, generosity, loyalty. And owing above all to his longevity, a miracle.[3]

The Knights of the Round Table illustrate the evolution of the image of the knight. Men of prowess in the twelfth century,

St George rescues the princess in this painting by Sano di Pietro,
15th century, tempera on panel.

at the turn of the thirteenth they became the heroes of courtly
love. As Duby has again shown, the starring role in knightly tales
in both periods was played by the young in search of castles, land
and women – even if, on this last point, Duby has been undercut
by the research of Christiane Marchello-Nizia, according to whom,
regarding courtly love, a woman would often be only the mask of
a young man: 'In this military society, wasn't courtly love actually
love for a man?' Marchello-Nizia reminds us of what Jacques Lacan

believed with regard to homosexuality: 'Courtly love has remained enigmatic.'[4]

It remains true that, as love dreamed or love lived, ideal love or carnal love, courtly love was an essential element in the imaginary of chivalry. Duby has also taught us to see that, as well as a social model, chivalry was a cultural model. The three essential goals of the *preux*, the brave and courtly knight, were adventure, honour and glory. Erich Köhler has described well what the chivalrous adventure truly was.

Every civilization has more or less close relationships with space. Medieval Christianity structured and controlled the European space. It created networks of hot spots (churches, places of pilgrimage, castles), but what is more, it criss-crossed a space of itinerant travelling in which, again, the forest was both dream and reality. In this perspective the knight was basically what most knights in the Middle Ages were: a knight errant. The Crusades were the most violent of those wanderings.

The medieval knight, both because of his adventurous nature as well as the non-hereditary nature of his title, was distinguished from the noble. Jean Flori has defined it this way:

> Throughout the Middle Ages, the nobility and chivalry intermingled their destinies; never, however, were the two terms synonymous, nor were their concepts equivalent; chivalry gradually saw its condition improve, attracting the nobility that had always controlled it, claimed ownership and control, and to a large extent, exclusivity over it. The noble 'corporation' of elite warriors in the thirteenth century thus became the elitist corporation of noble knights before being transformed, at the end of the Middle Ages, into an honorary noble brotherhood.

As often happens, chivalry did not escape the price of success, which was derision. Romaine Wolf-Bonvin has brought together two tales that are characteristic of the thirteenth century under the title *La Chevalerie des sots* (The Chivalry of Fools) (1990). It is a parody of the courtly romance *Le Roman de Fergus* and an erotic fabliau, *Trubert*. It is remarkable that the naive and foolish heroes, in Old French *nices*, were close to young Perceval at the beginning of Chrétien de Troy's romance. Isn't the orphan raised in solitude by his mother the exemplary child who through adventures would become a knight? In any case, this moral, under a Christian veneer, would constitute one of the important components of European mentality and ideology. Though he emerged out of innocence, in that world where marvellous heroes sometimes belonged, and as we will see with Melusina in the world of fairies, the knight could himself also be one of those fairy figures; there were '*fae*' knights.

Two important avatars mark the history of chivalry between the twelfth and fifteenth centuries. The first of these was the appearance of the military religious orders, the 'knights of Christ'. This was the culmination of Christianity's conversion to war. Before the eleventh century it was unthinkable that a figure might appear combining in himself the monk and the warrior, but this occurred within the context of the Crusades, when Pope Gregory VII (1073–85) introduced the expression *miles christi* (knight of Christ) onto the strictly military terrain. These new orders were created to defend the Holy Land, its Christian inhabitants and pilgrims. The Order of the Knights Hospitaller was created in 1113, followed in 1120 by the Poor Fellow-soldiers of Christ and the Temple of Solomon, or Knights Templar. Military orders also began to appear on the Iberian peninsula during the *Reconquista*: between 1158 and 1175 were founded the Order of Calatrava and the Order of Santiago and, in Portugal, there were the Friars of Santa Maria of Évora, the future Order of Avis. In the Holy Land a German brotherhood of hospitallers was founded at Acre, and became a military order in 1198, the Teutonic Knights of St Mary's Hospital at Jerusalem. Finally, a third region called upon these military orders, the pagan lands in northeastern Europe: the Livonian Brothers of the Sword was created in 1202–4 and the Teutonic Order settled in Prussia in 1230; the Brothers of the Sword and the Teutonic Order merged in 1237. After the fall of Saint-Jean-d'Acre, the Christian military orders, the Knights of Christ, retreated to Cyprus. The emerging Christian European monarchies, however, were becoming less and less tolerant of those hybrid monk-knights. Pressured by Philippe IV of France, in 1308 Pope Clement VII ordered the arrest of the Knights Templar throughout Christendom, and in 1312 the Council of Vienne suppressed the Order. In Poland, where the Teutonic Order had settled in Malbork, constant conflicts with the kings of Poland were marked by the spectacular victory of the Polish-Lithuanians over the Teutonics at Grunwald (Tannenberg) in 1410. Only the Knights Hospitaller survived, having retreated to Malta in 1530. They became the Knights of St John, devoted exclusively, even today, to humanitarian works.

The other avatar of the history of chivalry was the creation, in the fourteenth and fifteenth centuries, of decorations awarded by kings and princes to lay figures whom they wanted to distinguish or bring into their orbit. In 1330 Alfonso XI of Castile founded the first secular order of chivalry, the Order of the Band. Edward III of England created the famous Order of the Garter in 1348 and was followed by John II of France, who inaugurated the Order of the Star in 1351. The most famous of these creations was the Order of the Golden Fleece by Philip the Good, Duke of Burgundy, in 1430. These orders were similar to confraternities and, in that capacity, could be founded by mere knights. Thus Jean II le Meingre, also known as Boucicaut, founded the Enterprise of the Green Shield with the White Lady in 1399, intended to last for five years and dedicated to defending the honour of the ladies and damsels suffering from the violence of the Hundred Years' War. He also wrote a treatise exalting the old chivalrous values. These orders of chivalry demonstrated a nostalgia for the past, a rebirth of the Arthurian mystique. As Jean Flori has described, they tended to perpetuate 'a glorification of prowess, a sense of honour, generosity and greatness of soul'.

Within this chivalrous atmosphere a new theme in the world of marvellous heroes of medieval chivalry emerged and was promoted: the nine *preux*. This theme illustrates the thinking of scholars in the Middle Ages who tended to find a continuation of the same ideals among the three civilizations out of which medieval civilization emerged: Jewish civilization and the Old Testament; ancient pagan civilization; and medieval Christian civilization. And so they distinguished a group of nine *preux*: three Jews from the Old Testament – Joshua, Judas Maccabee and David; three pagans from antiquity – Hector of Troy, Alexander the Great and Julius Caesar; and three Christians from the Middle Ages – Arthur, Charlemagne and Godfrey of Bouillon, the first Latin king of Jerusalem in 1099. In England these were known as the Nine Worthies and their then somewhat old-fashioned status was mocked by William Shakespeare in the 1590s in *Love's Labours Lost*.

These nine *preux* appeared for the first time in a 1312 treatise by Jacques de Longuyon, *Les Voeux du paon* (The Vows of the Peacock). The popularity of tapestries in the fourteenth and fifteenth centuries, and the appearance of playing cards in the fifteenth century, ensured the success of these *preux*. Charlemagne became the King of Hearts in the tarot and on playing cards. The success of the theme of the

A knight of the Middle Ages in the modern world: Jean Reno in Jean-Marie Poiré's comedy *Les Visiteurs* (2002).

preux spread beyond the masculine world of chivalry. Female *preuses* appeared in the sixteenth century, thereby integrating into the world of chivalry women of action, whereas women hitherto had only passive roles in courtly love. The fifteenth and sixteenth centuries were therefore a time of chivalric excitement. A good example of this is seen in the success of a Catalan romance written by Joanot Martorell de Valencia and published posthumously in 1490, *Tirant lo Blanch* (Tirant the White). This imaginary knight was an important milestone on the road that went from Lancelot to Don Quixote. Cervantes saw it as 'the best book in the world', and the author states that he wanted to revive 'a taste for the feats and glorious deeds of the old and very virtuous knights'. In a preface to a recent French translation of *Tirant lo Blanch*, the great Peruvian novelist Mario Vargas Llosa declares that this ambitious romance deserves, as do very few others, to be called European:

Because half of Europe and the entire Mediterranean constitutes the setting which the hero of the story calls home, a man who feels as much at home in England as in Brittany, in Greece and in Spain, and recognizes no boundaries between human beings other than those of honour and dishonour, beauty and ugliness, courage and cowardice.[5]

However, new knights haunted the European imaginary of the fourteenth and fifteenth centuries, such as Amadís de Gaula, who appeared in the fourteenth century, and was the hero of a very popular romance by the Castilian Garci Rodríguez de Montalvo (*c.* 1450–1504). The Spanish and Portuguese conquistadores who conquered part of the New World in the early sixteenth century enjoyed reading this chivalrous literature in between their campaigns and battles. Understandably, we see the culmination of that literature in the masterpiece that is both the pinnacle of its exaltation and success, as well as an affirmation of criticism against a definitively outmoded ideal. That masterpiece is obviously Miguel de Cervantes' *Don Quixote* (1605–15).

Knights were resuscitated only through the scholarship of historians in the eighteenth and nineteenth centuries. A scholarly work, *La Chevalerie* by Léon Gautier (1894), reached a large audience in France and made chivalry popular there in the Belle Époque. Before then, the chivalrous ideal had inspired Bonaparte, who in 1802 created the Légion d'honneur, which has been maintained by all subsequent French governments. The most elevated title it bestows is that of *chevalier* (knight). The image of the gentleman, the new social hero combining the courtliness of nobles and the good manners of the bourgeois, which the English invented in the nineteenth century, has been associated with the image of the knight. Through the Knights of the Round Table, one finds knights in the imaginary of twentieth- and twenty-first-century film. The success of the three films in the series *Les Visiteurs* (dir. Jean-Marie Poiré, 1993, 1998 and 2016, and the original's English-language remake *Just Visiting*, 2001) proves that knights still make us dream, even if it is with a slightly ironic smile.

THE LAND OF COCKAIGNE

The Land of Cockaigne appeared as an imaginary land in an Old French fabliau from the beginning of the thirteenth century. This creation from the medieval imaginary was bequeathed to us through three manuscripts, the initial one from around 1250, and two copies from the beginning of the fourteenth century. The etymology of the word, which had not been seen until then, is unknown. The efforts of philologists to give it a Low Latin or Provençal origin and to link Cockaigne to cooking have remained fruitless. Cockaigne came out of the medieval imaginary fully formed.

The term in Old French, *Cocagne*, was quickly translated into English (*Cokaygne* or *Cockaigne*), Italian (*Cuccagna*) and Spanish (*Cucaña*). The Germans adopted another word, *Schlaraffenland*, whose origin is no better known. The fabliau of Cockaigne from the thirteenth century is made up of two hundred octosyllabic verses. It is the story of the anonymous author's voyage to an imaginary land undertaken as a penance imposed upon him by the pope. He discovers Cockaigne, 'a land of many marvels . . . blessed by God and the saints'. It is immediately defined by this marvellous characteristic: 'Qui plus i dort, plus i gagne' (the more one sleeps there, the more one earns). Sleep, then, is a source of profit. I believe this is a reference to usurers, who were criticized at the time for earning interest while they slept. The fabliau thus begins with an upending of thirteenth-century morality. The walls of the houses in this land are made of fish, 'bass, salmon, and shad', the rafters of sturgeons, the roofs of bacon, the floors (planks) of sausages; the wheatfields are enclosed by roast meat and ham; in the streets, fat geese are roasting, turning themselves on spits, endlessly seasoned with garlic. On all the roads, paths and streets there are tables covered with white cloths. Anyone can sit down and eat whenever they wish, fish or meat, venison or fowl roasted or in a pot, and everything is free. A river of wine flows through the land, a river in which cups, goblets of gold and silver, fill themselves. The river is made half of red wine, the best, such as that of Beaune or from abroad, and half of excellent white, such as that of Auxerre, La Rochelle or Tonnerre. All of that is free, too. And the people are not loutish, but act honourably and courteously. After this image of an abundance of food, an abundance whose quality matches the quantity, there are also the pleasures of a very special calendar. Months have six weeks; there are four Easters in the year, four Feasts of St John, four grape harvests, every day is a holiday and a Sunday; there are four All Saints Days, four Christmases, four Candlemas Days, four Shrovetides and Lent only once every twenty years.

The author returns to food, re-emphasizing that one can eat whatever and whenever one wants, because no one should be forced to go hungry. He had already spoken of unforbidden food: he now specifies 'que nus desfendre ne leur ose' (no one is forbidden who dares). One cannot help thinking of the slogan of May 1968: 'It is prohibited to prohibit.' It thus seems that the utopia of a society without interdicts goes back to the land of Cockaigne in the thirteenth century, a time that was concerned with other fundamental social issues, such as sexuality and work. And the fabliau of Cockaigne does not ignore those issues, either.

In concluding with food in the fabliau, let us point out that three days a week it rains warm boudin. Then the author turns to a fundamental critique of money, which becomes moot: 'This land is so rich that one finds purses filled with coins, including foreign gold coins, marabotins and bezants, everywhere in the fields, but they're worthless because everything is free in this land where one neither buys nor sells.' What the author of the fabliau is referring to here is the great explosion of the monetary economy in the thirteenth century.

Let's move on to sex. The women, both young and old, are very beautiful and every man takes the one he desires, and no one is offended. Each person satisfies his pleasure as he wishes, and at leisure. And the women aren't criticized; rather, they are honoured. And if it happens that a woman is interested in a man she sees, she takes him right in the street and is pleasured by him; people please each other. What is surprising here, it seems to me, is less the dream of a free sexuality, which one finds in texts of the time concerning the marvels of India, for example, than the surprising equality of women and men as seen in their sexual behaviour. In 1215, regarding marriage, the Church began to require and viewed the consent of the woman as equal to that of the man. That equality between the sexes in the fabliau is pushed to its extreme. The male Middle Ages was not always as uniformly misogynous as one might be led to believe.

One might expect the practice and praise of nudity, but that wouldn't be at all marvellous. The marvel is the suit of clothes. In this land there are clothes-makers who distribute each month various articles of clothing, dresses of brown, scarlet, violet or green fabric, or of good quality or coarse wool, or of silk from Alexandria, or of striped or camel hair cloth. There is a lot of clothing to choose from, both colourful or grey, and sometimes embellished with ermine; in this blessed land there are active shoemakers who turn out shoes with laces, boots and summer shoes well-formed to the shape of the foot, three hundred a day, if desired.

There is another marvel, the Fountain of Youth, which rejuvenates men and women. Every man, however old and bent he may be, every woman, however old and grey she may be, will return to the age of thirty (that is supposedly Christ's age when he began preaching).

Whoever enters that land and then leaves it is quite mad. 'That is what I did,' the author of the fabliau admits, 'because I wanted to go back to get my friends to bring them to that blessed land, but I no longer knew how to find it. If you are content on your land, don't seek to leave it, because in wanting change, one loses.'

The fabliau of Cockaigne probably escaped complete oblivion, first because it was cloaked in Christian references, but probably above all because its conclusion is a call not for revolt, but for resignation. It fulfilled the function of a description of utopia, which served as a challenge or a release. The lost paradise of the land of Cockaigne is a medieval and popular form of the elitist golden age of ancient philosophy. It was a dream of abundance that allayed the greatest fear of medieval populations, hunger; a dream of freedom that condemned the weight of all sorts of prohibitions, and of the domination of the Church; a dream not of laziness, but of *dolce far niente*, or at least of leisure at a time when work was promoted as honouring workers, when it served only to better subjugate them; finally, a dream of youth that was inspired by the low life expectancy of men and women in the Middle Ages. But what seems to me most notable in this text is the denunciation of the Church's and religion's framing of time. The dream of a calendar of happiness was one of the great dreams of the imaginary of societies.

In the end, the fabliau of Cockaigne is a dream of enjoyment. That, it seems to me, is enough to distinguish it radically from other contemporary heresies, which were in general rigorist heresies that condemned the flesh, material goods and pleasure, even more than did the Church itself. The land of Cockaigne would have horrified the Cathars.

It is not my place to weigh in on the argument that connects the land of Cockaigne to Paradise in the Koran. I personally don't believe in that connection. If there are resemblances, it seems one should seek their origins in similar pagan conceptions in both Eastern and Western history.

The utopia of the land of Cockaigne has made its way into the European imaginary. But this occurred in two phases. First, the

Rejuvenation in the magic water of the Fountain of Youth with
a return to nudity and amorous entertainments, bringing back youth
and its pleasures to aged men and women. Jaquerio Giacomo,
The Fountain of Youth, 15th century.

An obese man and an emaciated woman embody the opposition between the pleasures of the Land of Cockaigne and the asceticism imposed by the Church. Pieter Bruegel the Elder, *The Battle between Carnival and Lent*, 1559, oil on panel.

theme was integrated in the literature of amusing tales. The land of Cockaigne was fortunate enough to be picked up by Boccaccio in *The Decameron*. Then, the land of Cockaigne survived when it was combined with other controversial themes, the three main ones of which seem to be the Fountain of Youth, already present in the fabliau; the battle between Carnival and Lent, known as the Battle of Lent and Carnage, which emerged at almost the same time as the fabliau; and finally, the theme of an upside-down world. These themes can be widely found in the literature, art and imaginary of the sixteenth century. It is notable that the same great painter, Pieter Bruegel the Elder, painted the only great pictorial representation of the *Land of Cockaigne* (1567), favouring sweet nothing, sleep and physical prosperity, and the *Battle between Carnival and Lent* (1559). Modern criticism has seen the fabliau as either a 'dream of compensation', or a 'social utopia' (this is the opinion of the Czech historian František Graus), an 'anticlerical' utopia, a utopia 'of evasion' and, finally, a 'popular' or 'folkloric' utopia.

However difficult it may be to grasp the history of what is called popular culture, I think that that culture, which medieval Christianity had a tendency to denounce as pagan, was the historical framework of the time of the Land of Cockaigne. The thirteenth-century fabliau likely included pagan traditions. And in the modern era, probably beginning in the eighteenth century, the utopia of Cockaigne has anecdotally become a child's tale. Perhaps under the influence of the maypole (this question should be pursued), Cockaigne survived among rural and village communities by giving its name to an element of popular festivals, the *mât de cocagne* (the Cockaigne pole). At the top of the pole there is a prize, often in the form of food, a treat; someone, usually a child, must climb to the top to win the prize. The oldest mention of the Cockaigne pole seems to be in a chronicle called *Journal d'un bourgeois de Paris*, which notes that in 1425, a time when Paris was under the control of the English and the Burgundians, but still had fun:

On Saint-Leu-et-Saint-Gilles Day, which was Saturday 1 September, some parishioners proposed a new entertainment and provided it: they took a very long pole measuring 6 toises and planted it in the ground, and at the very top put a basket in which there was a fat goose and six coins, and they greased the pole very well; and then it was proclaimed that whoever could get to the goose by climbing without help would have the pole and the basket, the goose and the six coins; but no one, no matter how good a climber he was, could do it; but that evening, a young valet who had climbed the highest had the goose, but not the basket, or the coins, or the pole; this happened in front of Quincampoix [*sic*] on the rue aux Oies.[1]

The Cockaigne pole became a common part of country festivals. It illustrates the diversity of paths on which the marvellous myths that make up our imaginary have travelled.

MELUSINA

With Melusina, a marvellous heroine comes onto the stage. The medieval world of the imaginary might seem to have reflected the world of reality which, according to Georges Duby, was essentially a 'male Middle Ages'. Women, however, or some women at least, not only benefited from their social status, not only exercised great power, but quite often, admittedly as part of a couple, were very present in the medieval imaginary. We must not forget, too, that the Middle Ages was the period when Christianity in Europe imposed the all-powerful image of a woman, the Virgin Mary.

Melusina belongs to another interesting group of medieval female beings: fairies. Fairies for the men and women of the Middle Ages, as seen in texts from the High Middle Ages, were the descendants of the ancient Fates, whose Low Latin name *fatae* indicates their connection with destiny, *fatum*. Those fairies were gradually integrated into the Christian imaginary, which notably ranked them as either good or bad fairies. Though medieval fairies were essentially known for their good, or bad, deeds, people believed their activity in society was carried out most often within a couple. Melusina, in particular, was closely associated with procreation and with issues of lineage in the Middle Ages. But the complexity of most of these fairies, and notably of Melusina, justified a contrasting and even contradictory image of the woman and the couple in the Middle Ages. The same women, the same couples, were at the same time heroes of good and evil, and actors in stories that are both marvellously beautiful and marvellously terrible. No heroine illustrates better than Melusina the belief that no human being is entirely good or entirely bad.

Melusina appeared in Latin literature and then in vernacular texts during the twelfth century and the beginning of the thirteenth. Between the beginning of the thirteenth century and the end of the fourteenth, that woman fairy would gradually assume the preferred name of Melusina, which connected her to a great aristocratic family from western France, the Lusignans. In his critical work on the court of Henry II of England, *De nugis curialium* (On the Trifles of Courtiers), the cleric Walter Map tells the story of the young lord Henno, who has big teeth. In a forest in Normandy Henno encounters a young and very beautiful girl, wearing royal garb and crying. She tells him that she has escaped from a shipwreck while travelling to the king of France, whom she was to marry. Henno and the unknown beauty fall in love, they get married and she provides him with very lovely progeny. But Henno's mother notices that the young woman, who claims to be pious, avoids the beginning and the end of mass, and misses the sprinkling of holy water and communion. Intrigued, she cuts a hole in the wall of her daughter-in-law's room and catches her taking a bath in the form of a dragon, then resuming her human shape. When his mother tells him of this, Henno fetches a priest to sprinkle his wife with holy water. She then jumps through the roof with a great shriek and disappears into the sky. Walter Map claimed that, in his time, many descendants of Henno and his dragon-wife were still living.

In another well-known work, the *Otia imperialia*, from the beginning of the thirteenth century, the English cleric Gervase of Tilbury

Miniature of
Melusina from
Roman du
Mélusine, 1401.

tells the story of Raymond, lord of Rousset castle, who encounters
a beautiful lady on the banks of a river near Aix-en-Provence. She
is magnificently dressed and calls him by his name. Ultimately she
marries him, on condition that he should not try to see her naked,
for if he does he will lose all the material wealth she will bring him.
The couple are happy, become rich, enjoy excellent health and have
many beautiful children. But, ever curious, Raymond one day pulls
back the curtain behind which his wife is taking a bath in her room.
The beautiful wife turns into a snake and disappears in the bath water
forever. Only the wet nurses hear her at night when she returns, invis-
ible, to see her little children. Years later when the story was told
it would often be accompanied by illustrations showing Melusina
fleeing through a window or a roof as a winged dragon, and returning
in a visible form at night to see her small children.

The story is basically one of the transgression of a prohibition. It is believed that the most ancient heroine of a supernatural legend who marries a mortal under a certain condition and who, the day the pact is violated, disappears forever, can be found in Indo-European mythology in the nymph Urvaçi.

Apart from the symbolism of betrayal, however, which was particularly important in a feudal society founded on loyalty, the significance of the story seems to me to reside in the revelation of the prototypically and fundamentally diabolical figure, because that is indeed the meaning of the dragon or the snake, of the woman-animal who becomes a wife and mother. Above all, the myth of Melusina offers a terribly ambiguous explanation of success in feudal society. What Melusina brings to her mortal spouse is prosperity and wealth, as they were conceived by the West in the twelfth and thirteenth centuries: deforestation and, above all, the construction of castles, cities and bridges. At the same time, as an exceptional procreator, she embodies the great demographic surge of that time. Emmanuel Le Roy Ladurie and I have called her 'maternal and deforesting'. She is the fairy of feudalism. Her image seems predominately positive, she is good, active, fertile and ultimately unhappy in spite of herself, unhappy through betrayal. But the people of the Middle Ages were sensitive to her diabolical origins and saw in her a sort of Eve who had not been redeemed.

For the people of the Middle Ages, it was a great royal family who became kings of England in the twelfth century, the Plantagenets, counts of Anjou, who embodied the Melusinian lineage; originally powerful and diabolical with discord always active among them. There was constant conflict between Henry II and his wife, Eleanor of Aquitaine, and between the king and his sons. The eldest of these, Richard the Lionheart, according to Gerald of Wales at the beginning of the thirteenth century, had replied to those who were surprised by those internal disputes: 'How do you expect us to act? Aren't we the sons of the *Demon*?'

The structure of Melusina's story was formalized in the fourteenth century with three distinct stages: a fairy marries a mortal while demanding that he respect a prohibition; the couple enjoys great prosperity as long as the human husband keeps his promise; the pact is violated, and the fairy disappears, and with her the prosperity that she had brought in her dowry.

And so Melusina, according to Laurence Harf-Lancner's classification, is the prototype of loving fairies who bring good luck, as opposed to Morgane, the type of fairy who brings bad luck and takes their human lover or husband into the other world. As we have seen, however, Melusinian happiness cannot be completely detached from original sin, and Melusina is close to having the hybrid nature of a human being and diabolical animal.

At the end of the fourteenth century, at a particular conjuncture there occurred a great moment in the history of our heroine. Two romances were devoted to her, one in prose by the writer Jean d'Arras, written for Jean, duke of Berry, and his sister Marie, duchess of Bar; and one in verse, composed by the bookseller Coudrette.

The romances are founded on the transgression of the prohibition and on wrongdoing. Melusina's mother, Presine, had made her husband Elinas, king of Albany (Scotland), whom she had met hunting in a forest, promise not to be present when she gave birth. But Elinas violates his oath, and Presine, after bringing three daughters into the world – Melusina, Mélior and Palestine – disappears and goes to the island of Avalon with her daughters (here we see a blending with the Arthurian myth). When they are fifteen, the girls learn of their father's betrayal, and to punish him lock him up in a mountain. But they are in turn punished for the sentence they didn't have the right to inflict. Melusina's punishment is to be transformed into a snake every Saturday. If she marries a mortal, she will also become mortal, and if her husband sees her in the form she assumes on Saturdays, she will return to her torment. At a fountain Melusina meets Raimondin, the son of the count of Forez, who has just killed his uncle, the count of Poitiers, while hunting boar. Melusina promises that if he marries her she will get him out of this criminal accident and bring him happiness, wealth and lots of children. But he must swear never to try to see her on Saturdays. Once married to Raimondin, Melusina has forests cut down and constructs cities and fortified castles, beginning with the castle of Lusignan. They have ten children who become powerful kings, but all of them have a physical defect, a spot on their body, an animal mark and so forth. Coudrette is particularly interested in the sixth of those sons, Big-toothed Geoffrey, who demonstrates courage and cruelty, and who specifically sets fire to the monastery and the monks of Maillezais in Poitou.

In historical reality, however, the lords of Lusignan, within the framework of the Crusades, became kings of Cyprus and even carved out a kingdom for themselves in Anatolia, 'Little Armenia'. King Leo v of Lusignan was defeated by the Muslims who took his kingdom from him. He sought refuge in the West and attempted to form an alliance of Christian kings and princes to take back his kingdom. He died in Paris in 1393, without having achieved his goal. But his actions promoting an Armenian crusade were inscribed at the time within a broader expansion of Christendom toward a general crusade against Muslims. In 1396 an attempt ended in disaster at Nicopolis (now Nikopol), on the lower Danube, where the Crusader army was crushed by the Turks.

This crusading spirit permeated the romances of Jean d'Arras and Coudrette. The horizon of the Crusades in particular inspired the new and very developed episode whose heroine was Melusina's sister, Palestine. Punished for how she and her sisters had treated their father, Palestine was locked up with her treasure in the Canigou, a mountain in the Pyrenees. A knight from the Lusignan lineage would one day save her, be granted the treasure and use it to reconquer the Holy Land. This is what Big-toothed Geoffrey attempts to do for a long time in Coudrette's romance.

In Germanic literature and the German imaginary, however, there developed a masculine counterpart of Melusina. This was the Swan Knight, a supernatural figure who comes from the water and marries a mortal who must swear to respect a prohibition, which she violates, and he leaves her forever; he is the prototype of Richard Wagner's Romantic hero Lohengrin. Later we will again see the encounter between the Christian and Germanic imaginaries with the Valkyrie, and Wagner's role in their rebirth and reworking.

Melusina's great success in Europe was due to the German translation of Coudrette's romance in 1456 by Thüring von Ringoltingen, a high-level official from Bern. This translation was immediately successful thanks to the printing press (we know of eleven incunables, editions printed before 1500, seven of which are preserved) and to chapbooks. The chapbook *Historie der Melusine* was printed several times from the end of the fifteenth to the beginning of the seventeenth century in Augsburg, Strasbourg, Heidelberg and Frankfurt. What is more, there were many translations between the sixteenth and eighteenth centuries. The Danish translation published in Copenhagen in 1613 was very popular, and there were several Icelandic translations. There was a Polish translation in the sixteenth century, and a Czech translation that appeared in Prague at the end of the sixteenth century was reprinted five times. Two different translations in Russian appeared in the seventeenth century. The story of Melusina was extremely popular in Slavic countries, appearing in plays, and it spread into folklore and popular art. According to Claude Lecouteux, 'in central Europe, Melusina was transformed into a genie of the wind'.

In the Germanic cultural context, the Nuremberg mastersinger and shoemaker wrote his version of the story, *Die Melusina* (1556), in the form of a play in seven acts with twenty-five characters.

However, the actual terrestrial anchor of the myth of Melusina in the West disappeared in the sixteenth century. A seat of seigneurial resistance to royal power during the Wars of Religion, the castle of Lusignan was demolished by Henry III in 1575, and the so-called tower of Melusina, which had survived, was torn down as well in 1622. She survives in legend and as depicted by the Limbourg brothers flying over Lusignan in the illumination of *March* in the *Très Riches Heures du duc de Berry* (1411–16).

Melusina also benefited from the Romantic renaissance of the Middle Ages. Goethe retold the legend in a short story, 'Die neue Melusine' (1795–6), as did Ludwig Tieck in his *Sehr wunderbare Historie von der Melusina* (1800). More important, however, were the fragments from Achim von Arnim's adaptation, which he left unfinished when he died in 1831.

The legend of Melusina also benefited in the nineteenth and twentieth centuries from her similarity to a very popular aquatic fairy, Undine. To Friedrich de la Motte Fouqué's novella *Undine* (1811), from which came operas by E.T.A. Hoffmann (1816) and Albert Lortzing (1845), there would later be added the play *Ondine* (1938) by Jean Giraudoux, who was ever sensitive to the charm of Germanic legends. What unites Undine and Melusina is the myth of water. But Melusina is a cosmic heroine, much more broadly connected to nature. She is an aquatic heroine as well as a woodland one, and thanks to her dragon wings and her nocturnal flight, a celestial fairy. In the modern and contemporary era, a poetic vein, from Nerval to Baudelaire and André Breton, echoed the 'cries of the [medieval] fairy'. Melusina, a mother and a lover, haunts André Breton's *Arcane 17* (1944).[1]

The period closer to us has created a new image for Melusina. She has become 'a model of female existence', and the publishing house Melusine was set up in association with KVINFO, the Danish Centre for Research on Women and Gender.

Before becoming that feminist avatar, and thanks to two important characteristics, Melusina had a choice place in the European imaginary that came out of the Middle Ages. On the one hand, within relationships between humans and supernatural beings she combines both positive and negative elements. Benefactress fairies who bring wealth, children and happiness to humans, the Melusinas became diabolical. In the sixteenth century, the famous alchemist Paracelsus bequeathed to posterity that diabolized image of Melusina: 'Melusinas are desperate daughters of kings because of their sins. Satan takes them and transforms them into spectres.' The second characteristic is that Melusina is the essential element in a couple. She is manifest through a lover/spouse. She has achieved, perfectly, the fairy/knight couple with its successes and its failures. A fairy of feudalism, she has bequeathed to the European imaginary a sense of the success and failure of feudal society and the threats, in the longer term, of Western society. She has revealed to that society that the knight of the past and the capitalist of today, which provide it with prestige and success, are also in league with the Devil.[2]

The conception of Merlin, the son of a princess and a demon, from Robert de Boron's *Histoire de Merlin*, 13th century.

MERLIN

Though Arthur is probably a historical figure, Merlin is a product of literature. Merlin's success, however, was due to his early close association with Arthur. In the medieval and Western imaginary he is closely connected to the marvellous king, to the Knights of the Round Table and, more generally, to the heroic and marvellous world of chivalry.

Merlin was essentially a creation of Geoffrey of Monmouth, who in 1134 devoted his *Prophetiae Merlini* to him, portrayed him alongside Arthur in the *Historia regum Britanniae* (1138) and later wrote a *Vita Merlini* (1148). In the Middle Ages, Merlin was connected to a figure by the name of Ambrosius, who was described in the *Historia Brittonum* (eighth–ninth centuries) as a prophet, born without a father, who announced the future of the Britons. A Welsh popular oral tradition, moreover, brought a prefiguration of Merlin to life in the legend of Myrrdin Wyllt.

Three elements of his story give meaning to and a foundation for Merlin's success. First, there was his birth. Rather than having been born without a father, the Christian perspective soon made him the son of a mortal woman and an incubus demon. From that dubious paternity he inherited exceptional powers, but also a character of diabolical origin. He was indeed the type of hero who was torn between good and evil, God and Satan. The second element is that he was a prophet and put that gift to use in the service of King Arthur and the Britons. As we know from the history of Great Britain, the Britons were conquered by the Anglo-Saxons, who were conquered by the Anglo-Normans, who sought to gather all the ethnic legacies of the British Isles together, and Merlin became the figurehead of British nationalism. Finally, Merlin was believed to be the one who conceived of the Round Table, which he had Arthur create, and it was he who taught chivalrous virtues to the king and his elite knights.

An important new literary wave occurred when Merlin was appropriated by the Arthurian prose romances in the thirteenth century. We see a true evolution of Merlin's character first in Robert de Boron's *Merlin*, then in the *Vulgate Merlin*. The prophet Merlin was still closely connected to Celtic and pagan magic. It was he, for example, who was believed to have transported the huge stones of Stonehenge from Ireland to Salisbury Plain, and who appeared as a hero in moments of madness when he held back a laugh from the other world.

The Merlin of the thirteenth century was above all a magician and an interpreter of dreams, for example, filling the Arthurian kingdom of Logres with marvels. He became increasingly active, moreover, in the collective quest for the Grail. The *Livre du Graal* as its author defined it (*c.* 1230–40) was, according to Paul Zumthor, 'at the centre of Arthurian imagery; we might even say it was probably at the heart of the imaginary of the people of 1250'. According to Emmanuelle Baumgartner, the Grail at issue here was not divine, but diabolical, representing 'the diabolical desire that pushes man to know, to force secrets from God, to change destiny'. But that knowledge remained forbidden, and 'Merlin suffers endlessly in the perilous forest for having transmitted his secrets to humans and having delivered to the Lady of the Lake a power that God had given him only to remain the master of the game.' Merlin was thus the embodiment of the prophet who causes his own downfall, and the emblematic hero of the curse of prophesy in Christian ideology.

The ambivalence of his nature, however, which had previously been manifest by the struggle between good and evil in him, was henceforth revealed in the form of a conflict between his powers and his weakness. Indeed, he falls under the spell of a fairy who hypnotizes him, Niniene, who becomes Viviane, the Lady of the Lake. Viviane imprisons Merlin forever in a grotto or in a prison in the sky or under water. Merlin is also a hero connected to space, to the forest where he liked to live when he was free, to the air or to the water where he lived as a perpetual prisoner. The forest, which in the Middle Ages was considered to be Merlin's favourite dwelling place, was the forest of Brocéliande in Brittany, now known as the forest of Paimpont in Ille-et-Vilaine. Merlin is also a marker of place.

Merlin was a magician, and he did not abandon the world of prophesy. We find him at the origin of many political prophesies that agitated the West in the thirteenth and fourteenth centuries, mainly in Italy, where he sided with the Guelphs against the Ghibellines, specifically in Venice, where his image was influenced by the millennialist ideas of the disciples of Joachim of Fiore.

The later myth of the hero Merlin, alongside his gifts of prophesy and magic, emphasized less the theme of love, but more precisely that of the couple, a theme that greatly affected men and women in the Middle Ages. Early on, Merlin was smitten with Niniene, the daughter of a lord living in a castle in the forest of Briosque, and who was the godson of the goddess Diana. Niniene cast a spell on the wizard and he told her all his secrets; she could thus make him sleep when he wants to win her love, and ultimately imprisoned him in a castle in the forest of Brocéliande. Merlin ended his days a prisoner alongside his beloved behind a wall of air and leaves. According to Laurence Harf-Lancner, Niniene is Viviane, a 'Morgane-esque' fairy, that is, one who leads her lover into the other world. In the second version, the story of the loves of Merlin and Viviane is much darker. Viviane, a clear reincarnation of Diana, puts Merlin to sleep and has him placed in a tomb whose door she locks forever. This image of Merlin's amorous outcome was a pessimistic view, considering the way the men and women of the thirteenth century thought of the couple and love. Though Merlin became a member of the confraternity of smitten sages tricked by a woman, an outcome that might be – and has been – considered comedic, Merlin's love is above all presented, according to Harf-Lancner, 'as a fatal passion and his terrible end amounts to a punishment'.

In the sixteenth century Merlin's prophesies were definitively rejected. Rabelais had again made him a prophet in the service of King Gargantua, but the Council of Trent condemned Merlin's prophesies. While they were still mentioned in England, citations of his prophesies disappeared almost completely from continental literature after 1580.

Romanticism rediscovered Merlin. Karl Leberecht Immermann devoted an epic poem to him, *Merlin, eine Mythe* (1831), praised by Goethe as 'another Faust'. The most surprising work is Edgar Quinet's *Merlin l'enchanteur* (1860), which is sometimes reminiscent of Quinet's friend Jules Michelet and combines Quinet's taste for legends, his patriotism and his anti-clericalism. Quinet saw in Merlin the 'first patron of France', and the embodiment of the French spirit. Merlin's most intimate nature is solicited both by heaven and by hell, by a superhuman joy and a melancholy close to despair. He chooses as a place to reveal his marvels a village on an island in the Seine, which becomes Paris. Returning from Rome, he no longer recognizes France, which had entered into a new historical age – the Renaissance. He then 'becomes entombed' with Viviane and, in the words of Zumthor, 'he has nothing left but the power to populate his eternal sleep with dreams'. In fact, the Romantic Merlin was a condemnation, a distancing from the medieval Merlin.

Even more surprising was Merlin's revival within a return to ancient Celtic culture. The great agent of this revival was Théodore Hersart de la Villemarqué, whose collection of old Breton songs, *Barzaz Breiz* (Ballads of Brittany, 1839), caused much controversy as to how much of the work had been invented by the author. In the subtitle he explains the link between this Breton renaissance and the medieval imaginary: 'A popular tale of ancient Bretons preceded by an essay on the origin of chivalrous sagas of the Round Table'. There are four poems in *Barzaz Breiz* devoted to Merlin: 'Merlin in his cradle', 'Merlin the diviner', 'Merlin the bard' and the 'Conversion of Merlin'. Crowning his research and reflections on Merlin, Hersart de la Villemarqué in 1862 published the work that marks the apogee of Merlin's Romantic and Celtic revival: *Myrrddhin ou l'enchanteur Merlin: son histoire, ses œuvres, son influence*.

Merlin began to fade from literature after 1860, even if he can be found in the poems of Tennyson. The first half of the twentieth century saw a revival of Merlin, with Guillaume Apollinaire's *L'enchanteur pourrissant* (The Rotting Magician; 1909), a curious mixture of a play, poetry and novel, and Jean Cocteau's play *Les Chevaliers de la Table ronde* (1937). Merlin, like many of the heroes and marvels of the Middle Ages, came back to life in film and in the universe of children. The wizard with a white beard found his place in films about the Knights of the Round Table, notably providing

Cinematic depiction of Merlin in Walt Disney Studio's
The Sword in the Stone, 1963.

one of the most successful characters in Walt Disney's *The Sword in the Stone* (dir. Wolfgang Reitherman, 1963), based very loosely on the first part of T. H. White's trilogy *The Once and Future King* (1958).

Paul Zumthor believes that 'the legend of Merlin is on a path to extinction' and that Merlin is disappearing from the Western imaginary. But, in a history in which metamorphoses, resurgences and reappearances are so frequent, who would to dare say goodbye to the enchanting prophet?

POPE JOAN

Pope Joan was a scandalous heroine and at the same time a marvellous woman, a product of the medieval imaginary. The story appeared at the end of the thirteenth century, and I will summarize it from the wonderful book by Alain Boureau. Around 850, a woman from Mainz, but who was of English origin, dressed as a man in order to follow her lover, who was pursuing his studies and thus entering an exclusively male world. She herself became a student and succeeded so well that, after studying for some time in Athens, she went to Rome where she was warmly received. Her talents enabled her to rise in the hierarchy of the Curia, and she was ultimately elected pope. Her pontificate lasted more than two years, but was interrupted by a scandal: Joan, who had not renounced the pleasures of the flesh, became pregnant and died during a procession between St Peter's in the Vatican and the Archbasilica of St John Lateran, after giving birth in public. Various versions of the tale offered evidence and memories of the female pope. It was believed that this was the reason why the gender of the new pope was verified manually during their coronation, and that pontifical processions abandoned the direct path from the Vatican to St John Lateran, bypassing the basilica of San Clemente to avoid where she gave birth, and where that deplorable incident might have been commemorated by a statue and an inscription.

The female pope never existed. Joan is an imaginary heroine, but she was the object of both official and popular belief from 1250 to 1550, and belief in her existence was the origin of a ritual object and a ritual practice in the Christian Church during that period. She embodied the fear of women that was disseminated by the Church, and especially the fear that women might intrude into the Church itself. As part of the historical movement through which the Church ensured papal omnipotence, Joan was the reverse-image of a pope: a female pope. The Brazilian medievalist Hilário Franco Júnior, in his excellent book on medieval utopias, proposes seeing Pope Joan as the utopia of androgyny.[1] I, however, see the figure as a rejection of the other sex rather than its annexation. The female pope was imposed on the Church and on history in the thirteenth century. Alain Boureau has shown the role played in this fictional construction by what he calls the Dominican network. Pope Joan appeared first in the work of the Dominican Jean de Mailly (1243); then in *The Great Mirror* by the Dominican Vincent of Beauvais, St Louis's favourite encyclopedist (*c.* 1260). It was Martinus Polonus (from Troppau, now Opava, in Bohemia), a brother and pontifical penitentiary at the Dominican convent of Prague, who assured the fame of Pope Joan in his *Chronica Pontificum et Imperatorum* (Chronicle of Popes and Emperors; *c.* 1280):

After the aforesaid Leo [Leo IV], John, an Englishman by descent (*Johannes Anglicus natione/nativitate*) who came from Mainz, held the See two years, five months and four days, and the pontificate was vacant one month. He died at Rome. He, it is asserted, was a woman. And having been in youth taken by her lover to Athens in man's clothes, she made such progress in various sciences that there was nobody

Pope Joan giving birth, from a French manuscript of 1361.

equal to her. So that afterwards lecturing on the Trivium at Rome she had great masters for her disciples and hearers. And forasmuch as she was in great esteem in the city, both for her life and her learning, she was unanimously elected pope. But while pope she became pregnant by the person with whom she was intimate. But not knowing the time of her delivery, while going from St Peter's to the Lateran, being taken in labour, she brought forth a child between the Coliseum and St Clement's church. And afterwards dying, she was, it is said, buried in that place. And because the Lord Pope always turns aside from that way, there are some who are fully persuaded that it is done in detestation of the fact. Nor is she put in the Catalogue of the Holy Popes, as well on account of her female sex as on account of the foul nature of the transaction.[2]

Pope Joan appeared at the same time in the works of Dominican authors of *exempla*, such as Stephen of Bourbon and Arnold of Liège.

Around 1312, at a time when numbers were being assigned to papal rulers, another Dominican, Bartholomew of Lucca, a disciple of St Thomas Aquinas, in his *Historia ecclesiastica nova* attributed the number VIII to the female pope (thus she was John VIII), making her the 107th pope.

But in reality, during that period the Church definitively rejected women from institutional ecclesiastic responsibilities and sacramental functions. The *Decretum gratiani*, which established canon law about 1140, strictly barred women from functions in the Church. Regarding Pope Joan, at the end of the thirteenth century two more Dominicans wrote about the woman pope, Robert of Uzès in his visions and prophesies, and Jacopo da Voragine, the author of the *Golden Legend*, who in his *Chronica civitatis Januensis*, a chronicle of Genoa, described the horror of 'the pollution of the sacral by a woman':

That woman [*ista mulier*] undertook with presumption, pursued with falsity and stupidity and succeeded shamefully. That is, indeed, the nature of a woman [*natura mulieris*] which, before an action to undertake, has the presumption and audacity at the beginning, stupidity in the middle, and incurs shame at the end. And so the woman begins to act with presumption and audacity, but does not take into consideration the end of the action and what it involves: she thinks she has already done great things; if she can begin something great, she no longer knows, after the beginning, during the action, how to pursue with wisdom what had been begun, and this is due to a lack of discernment. And so she must finish in shame and ignominy what had been undertaken in presumption and audacity and pursued in stupidity. And thus, it appears clearly that a woman begins in presumption, continues in stupidity, and ends with ignominy.

The belief that Pope Joan was real resulted in the adoption for the pontifical liturgy of a new object and a new ritual. The object was a seat upon which the incoming pope sat during his coronation so that an attendant at the ritual could verify the new pope's 'parts' in order to avoid the risk of crowning another female pope. The ritual was the attendant's touching of the pope's body, in order to verify that he was indeed a man.

Mentalities and sensibilities, however, evolved regarding the female pope. The rituals and legends surrounding her became the stuff of folklore. In the nineteenth century, in the context of legends connected to the pope, the theologian Ignaz von Döllinger, in his work *Die Papst-Fabeln des Mittlalters* (Pontifical Fables of the Middle Ages), resituated the story of Pope Joan, which was put at the front of the book, within a series of legends regarding the popes of the Middle Ages. In the ninth century the *Cena Cypriani* (Feast of the Cyprian) describes a parody of a pontifical liturgy performed in the presence of the pope and the emperor, which led to actual carnivals being held in Rome: these were the Feasts of Testaccio, for which we have a description for 1256. At the same time, as Agostino Paravicini Bagliani has shown very well, there was increasing and impassioned interest in the body of the pope, in its real form as well as in its symbolic meaning.

Pope Joan endured the backlash against the evolution of the marvellous image of a woman. In this imaginary, we find the usual balancing act between good and evil, admiration and horror. Although the female pope was associated with a sorceress, she figured in that group of exceptional women whom Boccaccio portrayed in 1361 in his *De mulieribus claris* (On Illustrious Women). As Alain Boureau says: 'In 1361, Joan left the Church to enter literature and womanhood.'

The iconography of the female pope, however, developed on two levels. The historical and scandalous image appeared in miniatures, then in engravings, and focused on the scene of the birth. The hieratic and admirable image passed from carnival to allegory, and infused the tarot. A parodic vein inspired Rabelais in his *Tiers Livre* (1546). When Panurge wants to threaten Jupiter, seducer of women, with castration while he is napping, he cries out:

> I'll catch him in the nick . . . and would you know what I would do unto him? . . . I would . . . rid him of his Cyprian Cymbals, and cut so close and neatly by the breech, that there shall not remain thereof so much as one – so cleanly would I shave him, and disable him forever from being Pope, for *Testiculos non habet.*[3]

The allusion to the pontifical ritual is obvious.

Curiously, Lutheranism breathed new life into Pope Joan. The Lutherans were indeed delighted to pretend to believe in the reality of such a fine incarnation of the turpitude of the Roman Church. But soon, Calvinist scorn, then Rationalist criticism, ruined the myth of a historical Pope Joan. The *Encyclopédie* ranked the female pope among old wives' tales. And Voltaire, in the *Essai sur les moeurs* (Essays on the Manners of Nations), wrote regarding the assassination of John VIII in 882: 'It is no more true than the story of Pope Joan.' The story of Pope Joan was brought back briefly in Dietrich Schernberg's play *Fraw Jutta* (*c.* 1480), although it was not published until 1565.

The French Revolution was only mildly interested in the theme of the female pope, within a general movement criticizing religion and the Church. *La papesse Jeanne*, an *opéra-bouffon* to a libretto by A.J.B. Defauconpret, was turned down by two theatres in Paris but eventually performed at the Théâtre Molière in 1793 and was printed that year. A duet between Jeanne and Cardinal Maffeo, one of her two cardinal lovers, set to a tune from Dalayrac's *Les deux petits Savoyards*, ends with Jeanne making her exit to the revolutionary song 'Ah! ça ira':

When on the forehead of Jeannette
The tiara will shine
It's our choice, my chickadee
Yes, all of Rome will applaud
Oh. Oh. Oh. Oh. Ah. Ah. Ah. Ah.
Look at the pretty little pope.
Next to the beauty that adorns you
We will soon see eclipsed
The vain shine of the tiara.
Ah, all will be well, all will be well, all will be well.

The story of the female pope, however, still seemed popular, at least in Rome. Stendhal, in his *Promenades dans Rome* (1830), in which he in large part copies *Un nouveau voyage d'Italie* written by Maximilien Misson in 1694, says:

> Who would believe that there is today in Rome people who attach much importance to the story of Pope Joan? A quite considerable figure and who claims to know attacked me this evening on Voltaire who, according to him, would have allowed himself much impiousness on the occasion of Pope Joan.

Pope Joan became popular again at the end of the nineteenth century and in the twentieth as a 'curiosity of Western history'. A satirical novel, *Pope Joan*, published in Athens in 1886 by the Greek author Emmanuel Rhoïdes seems to have sparked that revival, even though he was excommunicated by the Greek Orthodox Church and, from the Catholic standpoint, the book was attacked by Jules Barbey d'Aurevilly. Rhoïdes' novel was very popular and translated into the main European languages, including French (by Alfred Jarry, published posthumously in 1908) and English (by Lawrence Durrell, 1954). It was thought that Georges Bernanos' detective novel *Un Crime* (1935) was based on the story of Pope Joan. Joan even made it to the big screen. *Pope Joan* (dir. Michael Anderson, 1972) was a commercial failure despite a fine cast led by the beautiful Swedish actress Liv Ullmann. The first attempt to recut the film into one that works was renamed *The Devil's Imposter* in the U.S. and a second followed in 2009, shorn of 20 minutes and now called *She Who Would Be Pope*. Another version of the story, *Die Päpstin* (dir. Sönke Wortmann), was also released in 2009, based on the novel *Pope Joan* (1996) by Donna Woolfolk Cross. Pope Joan is one of the guests at the dinner party that forms the first act of Caryl Churchill's play *Top Girls* (1982).

Pope Joan has also been seen in works that were particularly well received in the United States, notably those by the French feminist Luce Irigaray, which delve into the tumultuous relationship between the Church and women throughout history, and in particular in the Middle Ages. It is probable that Pope Joan will remain in the background of ecclesiastic obsessions as long as the Vatican and part of the Church keep women at a distance from ecclesiastical institutions and sacramental functions. The image of that scandalous heroine, Pope Joan, is probably still vivid in the Vatican consciousness today.

REYNARD

Reynard is one of the most original creations of the Middle Ages, even if a prototype had already appeared in the ancient fables of Aesop.

Reynard has counterparts in most folklores and cultures around the world, because he embodies a precise social and cultural type: the trickster or deceiver. In the medieval and European imaginary Reynard represents an aspect that the ancient Greeks had defined as *métis*, though there was no acknowledged corresponding figure.[1] Reynard also represents the complex nature of relationships between humans and animals. In this book, alongside the unicorn, he represents the real animal as opposed to the legendary animal; he is a member of a universe that fascinated the men and women of the medieval West, one that was abundantly present in their culture and imaginary: the universe of animals. In Genesis, God offers animals to man since, after they are created, God asks man to give them names, thereby making man participate in their creation and legitimizing man's domination over them. Following this scriptural origin, humans encountered animals in everyday life in feudal society, whether they were house animals, almost a part of the family, animals who worked in the fields, elements of a fundamental rural world, or came from the universe of the hunt, a prestigious guarded seigneurial space. Above all, very early on in the High Middle Ages, an intense symbolic dimension was added to that everyday familiarity. The entire moral life of people, both individually and collectively, was reflected in the animal world. For the men and women of the Middle Ages animals were essential symbolic representations of fear or pleasure, damnation or salvation.

In that animal society, both real and imaginary, the fox held a special place. In addition to what he essentially represented – the embodiment of ruse and the ambiguity of beings – in the medieval and European imaginary Reynard was involved in two significant relationships. On the one hand, he had an adversary, a rival, an alter ego, Ysengrin the wolf; on the other, he could not be separated from the society in which he lived, a mirror of monarchical feudal society. Within that society he had a privileged relationship with the lion, the king. Reynard, always complex, always ambiguous, was sometimes the vassal and servant of the lion, and sometimes his opponent, and ended up being the usurper.

Reynard entered into the medieval imaginary with a handicap. He didn't appear much in the Bible, but one scriptural reference is usually applied to him: 'Take us the foxes, the little foxes, that spoil the vines: for our vines have tender grapes' (Song of Solomon 2:15). Reynard then appeared as part of the two antagonists – wolf and fox – in a clerical poem from the end of the eleventh century, the *Ecbasis cujusdam captivi* (The Escape of a Certain Prisoner). It is the story of a calf (the symbol of a monk) who flees blindly through the Vosges in front of a vicious and murderous wolf, who symbolizes laymen. The work is situated within the context of Gregorian reform and the issue of investitures, and it immediately established the polemical framework in which Reynard's story would be instructive. Around 1150 the *Ecbasis* inspired the *Ysengrimus*, an animal epic in verse composed by a monk or a priest from Ghent. The theme of this epic is the conflict that puts the fox Reynard in opposition to his uncle, the wolf Ysengrin, who is constantly humiliating him; in the end Ysengrin is eaten by pigs. *Ysengrimus* thus establishes an opposition that would be fundamental in the *Roman de Renart*, the one between the talented Reynard and the villainous wolf, who is both an imbecile and cruel. If I had wanted to introduce an anti-hero among the heroes in this book, it would certainly have been the wolf, the great victim of the European imaginary since medieval times. The wolf in the Middle Ages was seen as both ferocious and stupid. In addition, *Ysengrimus* introduced several scenes that would become famous episodes in the *Roman de Renart*, including the stolen ham, fishing and consulting Reynard the doctor.

Despite this legacy and borrowings, the *Roman de Renart*, which would definitively turn Reynard into one of the heroes of the medieval imaginary, is an entirely different beast. It is a unique work in the history of literature, because the *Roman de Renart* was assembled by clerics, then historians of literature, from more or less independent fragments written by multiple authors at various times between around 1170 and 1250, constituting what are called its 'branches.'

Before watching Reynard in action, I should first point out that, while there are many different species of fox, the fox of the romance and consequently of the imaginary was the one that naturalists call *Vulpes vulpes*, the red fox. In the Bible the colour red was the colour of evil, so the colour of Reynard's coat has contributed more than a little to the negative aspect of his image. Finally, let us note that during the twelfth century, in Old French and in the animal

The battle between Reynard and Ysengrin in a French manuscript,
13th century.

onomastic, the French term *goupil* (from the Latin *vulpes*) gradually
faded before the Germanic term for fox, probably deriving from a
first name, Reinhart or Reginard.

Through the various branches of the *Roman de Renard* we can
reconstitute a more or less continuous plot, as Robert Bossuat and
Sylvie Lefèvre, whom I am following here, have done. Reynard plays
a series of mean tricks on the rooster Chantecler, on the titmouse,
on the cat Tibert, on the crow Tiécelin and, above all, on the wolf
Ysengrin. He humiliates the wolf cubs, sleeps with his wolf wife,
Hersant, and rapes her in front of him. Ysengrin and Hersant go
to the court of the king, Noble the lion, to seek justice. Reynard
avoids the sentence the court has imposed by swearing he will right
his wrongs. And he escapes a trap set by Hersant and the dog. He
humiliates the wolf more than ever using tricks that could lead
to his hanging. Ignoring another summons by Noble's court, he
eats Coupé the chicken. He finally surrenders to the court on the

insistence of his cousin Grimbert, the badger. Sentenced to the gallows, he is released when he swears he will carry out a pilgrimage to the Holy Land. Once free, he throws away his cross and pilgrim's staff and flees. The king unsuccessfully besieges him at his subterranean castle Maupertuis ('bad opening', designating the opening to the burrow). Reynard commits a thousand bad deeds and tricks, seduces the lioness, the queen, and tries to usurp the lion's royal throne. Mortally wounded in the end, he is buried with great pomp to the joy of his victims, but comes back to life, ready to begin all over again.

That is the hero Reynard, both admired and detested, the embodiment of progressively negative traits ranging from intelligence to trickery and betrayal, through the use of ruses. He was instrumental in glorifying trickery in medieval and European culture more than any other ambiguous hero of that imaginary in which, as we have seen, there was no perfect hero (perfection is not of this world). More than any other figure he elicits the questions: is he good? Is he evil?

By the way Reynard acts at the animal court, he forces one to consider trickery in its social and political context. Like all heroes of the Middle Ages, he was connected to a place; he was anchored on the earth, and Maupertuis was a sort of anti-castle. Above all, perhaps, Reynard reveals a fundamental element of the medieval imaginary more forcefully than does any other hero: the impassioned and frenzied search for food. A tale of tricks, the *Roman de Renart* is even more perhaps an epic of hunger. Reynard was also an emblematic figure in relationships between men and women. Reynard was indeed the embodiment of the feudal male who in his interactions with women oscillated between seduction and violence.

Finally, as it advanced into the thirteenth century, Reynard's image took on an increasingly satirical aspect, leaving farther and farther behind the strictly animal traits of his beginnings, and becoming more diabolical. He was more often identified with a *figura diaboli*, and embodied that fundamental image of the Devil that became stronger throughout the Middle Ages; he became the trickster.

The *Roman de Renart* spread widely throughout European culture and in the various vernacular languages that were developing from the thirteenth to the sixteenth centuries. First, in French, were *Renart le Bestourné* by Rutebeuf, *Renart le Nouvel* by Jacquemart Gielée and *Renart le Contrefait*, by a cleric from Troyes at the beginning of the fourteenth century. All of these texts accentuate the satirical nature of the story. It was the Germanic and Flemish vein that was most developed, seen mainly in the version *Reinhart Fuchs* by Heinrich der Glichesaere at the end of the twelfth century, but also in the Flemish poem *Van den Vos Reinarde* and its successor, *Reinaerts Historie*. An Italian version, *Rainardo e Lesengrino*, appeared in Venice in the thirteenth century. Finally, William Caxton printed his own English translation from Flemish, *The History of Reynard the Fox*, at his press in Westminster in 1481.

As Claude Rivals has pointed out, after the twelfth century, the second great moment when Reynard entered the European imaginary was the classical era of the seventeenth and eighteenth centuries, when Reynard 'was divided between the fiction of the fabulist and the knowledge of the narrator'. The fabulist was La Fontaine, who put Reynard front and centre in 24 of his fables. Following the taste of the times, Reynard was still the trickster, the wily one, but the fabulist above all wanted to humanize the animal and what he symbolized, seeing in the defects that had made him detestable in the Middle Ages, weaknesses that made him human, because he sought to substitute strength of mind for brute force, and, in a pitiless society, attempted to hold on to his freedom. The naturalist Georges-Louis Leclerc, Comte de Buffon, obviously aimed to describe the animal in a scientific, neutral and impartial way, but even he was unable to avoid sketching a portrait in which his feelings show through:

> The fox is famous for his wiles and in part deserves his reputation. What the wolf does only through strength, he does through skill and succeeds more often . . . Delicate as well as circumspect, ingenious and cautious, even to the point of patience, he varies his behaviour, he has means of reserve that he can use when needed . . . He is not a wandering animal, but a domiciled animal.[2]

The legacy of the *Roman de Renart* is seen most clearly in German-speaking lands. The poem by Heinrich der Glichesaere influenced a telling of the story in prose as *Reineke der Fuchs* (1752) by Johann Christoph Gottsched, which in 1794 inspired Goethe's *Reineke Fuchs*, a poem in twelve parts. Goethe had been very influenced by Johann Gottfried Herder, who saw in the story the very model for the German epic, and in Reynard 'nothing other than the Ulysses of all Ulysses'. The fever that embraced Reynard in the Romantic era was pursued into the twentieth century, to the point that a collector named Friedrich von Fuchs established his own Reineke-Fuchs-Museum in Linden-Leihgestern.[3] Furthermore, in 1998 the Stadsmuseum Lokeren in Belgium, in collaboration with the University of Lausanne and the Catholic University of Nijmegen, organized exhibitions to celebrate the five-hundredth anniversary of the oldest German incunable of *Reynaert*, which was printed in Lübeck in 1498.

Reynard was also a hero in twentieth-century French literature, which reacted against how the character had been stifled in the nineteenth century by the socialist utopian Charles Fourier, who saw Reynard as a model for all that is rotten and base, offering instead an apologia for the dog and a rehabilitation of the wolf. Many works of French literature were devoted to Reynard, 'the dual and ambivalent being that fascinates, situated between nature and culture, between good and evil'. Louis Pergaud's collection of short stories *De Goupil à Margot* won the Prix Goncourt in 1910. The novelist Maurice Genevoix, with his characteristic love of nature, published *Le Roman de Renart* (1968), with illustrations by André Pec. Jean-Marc Soyez brought out a remarkable novel, *Les Renards* (1986), dealing with poaching. Saint-Exupéry, in his famous philosophical tale *Le Petit Prince*, has the fox speak with the young hero.

Indeed, in the second half of the twentieth century Reynard found a new means of expression to bring himself back to life: children's books. *Der Findefuchs* by Irina Korschunow, for example, was published in Munich in 1982 and has been translated into French as *Renardeau* (1984) and English as *The Foundling Fox* (2005). The Japanese writer Akiko Hayashi's book about a toy fox has appeared in English as *Aki and the Fox* (1991) and *Amy and Ken Visit Grandma* (2006) and in French as *Ken, le renard d'Aki* (1989). Henri Bosco's *Le Renard dans l'île* (The Fox on the Island, 1962) and Jacques Chessex's *Le Renard qui disait non à la lune* (The Fox Who Said No to the Moon, 1974), with illustrations by Danièle Bour, also found young audiences. The fox for adults from the medieval imaginary became a fox for children.[4]

No less surprising was Reynard's destiny in the world of film. Reynard was first the hero of the amazing *The Tale of the Fox* by Ladislav Starevitch, who told the main episodes of the romance using stop-go animation. Although the animation was complete by 1930, technical problems synchronizing sound meant that its release was delayed until a German version appeared in 1937. The spirit of the film is comedic and libertarian; it shows 'the resistance of an independent mind to the pretention of the powerful in governing all aspects of existence'.

Another surprise is finding Reynard playing Robin Hood in the world of Disney cartoons. In the 1973 cartoon *Robin Hood* (dir. Wolfgang Reitherman), Reynard plays Robin (voiced by Brian Bedford) and wears the felt hat Errol Flynn wore in the 1938 film by Michael Curtiz. Finally, what might be the most surprising is that the Spanish word for fox, *zorro*, became the name of one of the most extraordinary and popular film heroes. Zorro evolved into a myth thanks to Douglas Fairbanks, who played the role in the *The Mark of Zorro* (dir. Fred Niblo, 1920), which takes place in New Mexico and California in the years before 1848. The myth of Reynard became associated with a new, oversized realm of the imaginary, beyond Europe this time, the imaginary of the Wild West, where Zorro-Reynard underwent another metamorphosis, which transformed him into a masked lawman.[5]

ROBIN HOOD

Robin Hood may have existed, but he is essentially a literary creation celebrated in ballads from the thirteenth to the fifteenth centuries. He is associated primarily with the English imaginary, but also has a place in that of Europe.

Robin Hood introduced into the European imaginary, heir to that of the Middle Ages, a representative figure, the outlaw, the rebel lawman, in an original setting – the inhabited forest. The figure may have actually lived in thirteenth-century England, but his existence was assured through literature, and his oldest mention is found in *Piers Plowman*, a Middle English poem written between 1360 and 1390 by William Langland.[1] Robin Hood is cited in it as a hero of popular ballads, although we have texts of ballads dedicated to Robin Hood only from the fifteenth and sixteenth centuries. Robin Hood thus appeared in the iconography of medieval miniatures quite belatedly. He seems to have first appeared in the social history of England in the thirteenth century, and primarily at the end of the fourteenth century, echoing the popular revolts and religious conflicts of the 1380s. Robin Hood was the defender of the humble and the poor, he was the man of the forest, the leader of a group. He was always flanked by a faithful companion (Little John) and a truculent monk (Friar Tuck). Romanticism added a lady friend, Maid Marian.

Robin Hood
illustrated in
the 16th century.

Robin Hood had an enemy who represented political and social power, the pitiless and unpopular Sheriff of Nottingham. Robin lived and carried out his plans most often in Sherwood Forest, in Nottinghamshire. He was an archer, a symbolic activity that contributed to ensuring his mythical image. He thus possessed that emblematic accessory, the longbow, in contrast to the noble knight on horseback armed with a lance and sword. Robin Hood was an ambiguous figure, just like all heroes of the Middle Ages, existing between the law and thievery, right and wrong, revolt and service, between the forest and the court. With his band of men he stole from the rich to feed and clothe the poor, coming to the aid of the unarmed and powerless who were attacked by travelling knights. The titles of the principal ballads devoted to him in the fifteenth and sixteenth centuries describe his adventures well: 'Robin Hood and the Monk', 'Robin Hood and the Potter', 'Robin Hood and the Sheriff', 'The Tale of Robin Hood' and 'Robin Hood's Death'.

The sixteenth-century fashion of ballads devoted to him continued up to the time of Shakespeare, whose work is the ultimate and most striking expression of the Middle Ages. *As You Like It* (1598–1600) is a transposition of the story of Robin Hood. The hero, Orlando, has been stripped of his land and his title by his brother, and seeks refuge in the Forest of Arden with other exiled noblemen.

The myth of Robin Hood offers an exceptional example of an imaginary figure. We have seen that our heroes and marvels were often relaunched in the Romantic period, but in the case of Robin Hood, he was born again in Romantic literature. Robin Hood's new father in the modern and contemporary imaginary was the Scottish novelist Walter Scott, who gave Robin Hood a newly defined history in his novel *Ivanhoe* (1819).[2] Scott's genius was to place this legendary figure into a defined setting at the end of the twelfth century, which is one of the most impassioned periods in English history. Robin, under the name of Locksley, with his band of men protects the Saxons who were being oppressed by the conquering Normans, and joins forces with Richard the Lionheart against his brother John, who has seized the throne while the king was held captive during his return from the Crusades. Even more important, he saves the king who has returned to England incognito. The scene where Robin reveals his identity to the king is one of the greatest moments in the novel. Scott also resolves the problem of Robin's robberies, which the king readily pardons because of his services. Robin declares: 'Call me no longer Locksley, my Liege, but know me under the name, which, I fear, fame hath blown too widely not to have reached even your royal ears – I am Robin Hood of Sherwood Forest.' And King Richard exclaims: 'King of Outlaws, and Prince of good fellows! Who hath not heard a name that has been borne as far as Palestine? But be assured, brave Outlaw, that no deed done in our absence, and in the turbulent times to which it hath given rise, shall be remembered to thy disadvantage.'[3]

Robin Hood was also hugely popular with the American public. In particular, he became the idol of American children thanks to the work of the author and illustrator Howard Pyle, who turned him into the hero of his illustrated children's book *The Merry Adventures of Robin Hood* (1883). The very successful comic opera *Robin Hood*, by the American composer Reginald De Koven (1859–1920), was first performed in Chicago in 1890 and received many New York revivals (when taken to London in 1891 it was renamed *Maid Marian*). Perhaps the American success of Robin Hood comes from his more or less conscious association with the heroes of westerns.

In any event, a century after Walter Scott it was film and television that immortalized Robin Hood. Two big films in which the hero is played by a Hollywood star ensured that success. There was first the 1922 silent film by Allan Dwan starring the athletic Douglas Fairbanks. But it was really *The Adventures of Robin Hood* (1938), begun by William Keighley and completed by Michael Curtiz, with Errol Flynn in the title role and Olivia de Havilland as Lady Marian Fitzwalter, that sealed his fame.[4] More than fifty years on it was this image of the outlaw that was parodied in Mel Brooks's *Robin Hood, Men in Tights* (1993). Robin Hood has been the hero of many films, including Walt Disney's cartoon (1973), which has been mentioned earlier in relation to Reynard. These films often had evocative titles, such as *The Story of Robin Hood and his Merrie Men* (dir. Ken Annakin, 1952), and *Robin Hood, Prince of Thieves* (dir. Kevin Reynolds, 1991), starring Kevin Costner. Three British TV series have used Robin

Robin Hood, romantic national hero, as illustrated in Rose Yeatman Woolf's *Robin Hood and his Life in the Merry Greenwood* (1910–20).

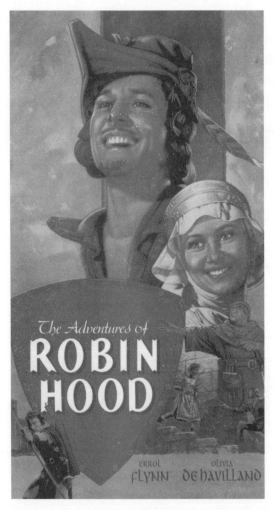

Errol Flynn as
Robin Hood and
Olivia de Havilland
as Maid Marian in
*The Adventures of
Robin Hood* (dir.
Michael Curtiz,
1938).

Hood to mirror the changes in post-war society: *The Adventures of Robin Hood* (1955–60) with Richard Greene was clean-cut and studio-bound; *Robin of Sherwood* (1984–6), with Michael Praed, followed by Jason Connery, was post-hippy and mystical, looking back to medieval legends; while Jonas Armstrong (2006–9) was a young and flawed survivor of the Crusades (shades of Iraq), whose northern accent marks him out as a man of the people. Returning to film, Robin Hood is such a fascinating hero that he inspired a work that highlights not his bandit side, but shows him as an ageing man still in love and still fighting against the schemes of the evil sheriff; this is the theme of the very original and elegiac *Robin and Marian* (dir. Richard Lester, 1976) with Sean Connery and Audrey Hepburn. Since the Middle Ages, Robin Hood has been a hero of the imaginary for all ages and for all time.

The song of Roland, after a 13th-century manuscript.

ROLAND

Roland is a historical figure about whom we know almost nothing. He is known only by his presence in Einhard's *The Life of Charlemagne* from the early ninth century.

Einhard introduces Roland as prefect of the march of Brittany. Very early on he was understood to be Charlemagne's nephew, but the dark legend that developed about Charlemagne made Roland the offspring of his incestuous relationship with his sister. Thus the hero Roland, fearless and beyond reproach, survived despite the stain of his birth. Roland was no more immaculate than any of the other heroes of the medieval imaginary. Of all the heroes presented here he was, moreover, the one most closely connected to a national culture, in his case, that of France. Created by a literary work, the *Chanson de Roland*, he is the product of what has been called 'the founding text of our literature, our culture, and our history, the first creative manifestation of our language'.[1]

The *Chanson de Roland* appeared around 1100 'from the synthesis of old, undefinable elements, and new creative elements in the mind and art of a poet who has been called Turold ... The appearance of this masterpiece, the fruit of a brilliant initiative, put to rest earlier songs and tales.'[2] The author, Turold, was believed to be an Anglo-Norman cleric who is depicted on the Bayeux Tapestry, and around 1125 William of Malmesbury wrote that he had been a jongleur who coached Norman troops to recite a *Cantilena Rolandi* at the Battle of Hastings, which delivered England to William the Conqueror. There was probably a primitive version of the *Chanson de Roland* reflecting the national spirit of the Capetian kingdom around the middle of the twelfth century, but the manuscript on which the modern edition of the *Chanson* is based is an Anglo-Norman and modernized version (*c.* 1170–80), preserved in the Bodleian Library, Oxford, and made by someone in the entourage of Henry II of England.

The *Chanson de Roland* tells of an episode that probably had a historical basis in Charlemagne's campaign of 778 against the Saracens in Spain, particularly Marsile, king of Saragossa. The bellicose Roland and the pacifist Ganelon cannot agree on strategy, but Charlemagne decides to make peace with Marsile. Ganelon, out of hatred for Roland, treacherously incites Marsile to attack the rearguard of Charlemagne's army, which had been entrusted to Roland. The unexpected attack occurs in the Pyrenees at the col de Roncevaux where a huge Saracen army overcomes the little Christian army commanded by Roland, assisted by his companion Oliver and Archbishop Turpin. They need to call on the emperor to rescue them, but Roland, out of pride, refuses, and it is too late when he finally decides to sound his horn to summon Charlemagne. Roland and his companions can only defend themselves valiantly and they are killed to the last man. Charlemagne arrives too late and can do nothing but give them a decent burial. The Saracens are defeated and Saragossa is captured. Roland's fiancée, the beautiful Aude, dies when Charlemagne returns to Aix-la-Chapelle (Aachen) and tells her of Roland's fate. The old emperor, crying, states that he will have to begin fighting the Saracens again.

The *Chanson de Roland* is infused with the spirit of the Crusades, but over the centuries it wasn't that spirit that left the strongest imprint on the imaginary. Its main legacy was the figure of Roland, who became the model of the Christian knight, and later, as we will see, especially French knights.

Roland's character in the *Chanson* develops through his relationships with four individuals. Most notable is the contrast between Roland and his dear friend Oliver, whose behaviour and nature, however, are very different. According to the *Chanson*, 'Roland is *preux*, but Oliver is wise.' Roland is impulsive, which allowed later literature to turn him into a hothead. Oliver is more composed. In the end, the perfect knight who emerges from the *Chanson* would be a combination of the two, in whom moderation tempers excess. What is interesting is that it was the excessive character that won out in the European and notably the French imaginary. It remains true, however, as Pierre Le Gentil has noted, that the Roland of the *Chanson* was a character who had his weaknesses. He was above all human, and he thus evolved in that humanity which, as we have seen, was shared by all the heroes of the medieval and European imaginary.

Another relationship is that of Roland and Charlemagne. It has been stressed that the *Chanson de Roland* is a poem of vassalage, expressing par excellence the feudal spirit through the relationship between a lord and his vassal. Images of Roland and Charlemagne are closely associated in the stained glass of Chartres Cathedral. It seems to me that it is the figure of the king (here, an emperor) that is dominant. Charlemagne is not an autocrat: he consults, takes advice, weighs the risks, bemoans his obligations. He shows that in the European imaginary supreme political power was not an absolute power, which makes the absolutist period of monarchical power in the sixteenth and seventeenth centuries not the culmination of European political ideology, but a parenthesis in that evolution.

Along with Oliver and Charlemagne, Roland has a close relationship with Archbishop Turpin. That character, who would also leave an important literary legacy, obviously represents the Church. The duo show how immutably connected are the lay and the clerical, the ideal being that relationships between those who pray and those who fight could be as good as that between Roland and Turpin. Finally, Roland is also representative of relationships between the sexes, but Aude has an ambiguous place in the *Chanson*. She is the companion whom the hero aspires to marry, and the poem essentially ends with her death, but otherwise the plot plays out almost entirely among men. This is indeed Georges Duby's 'male Middle Ages'. The hero Roland is also distinguished by the possession and use of objects marked with a sacral character. His sword, named Durandal, is like a living being and Roland's inseparable companion. The horn, or olifant, that he carries on his belt is also a sacral object, a producer of sounds to generate help, which has been compared to a sonorous horn of plenty.

Roland also fits the traditional image of the hero through the importance given to his death and tomb. The *Chanson* is really just a long death agony, and Roncevaux is the most prestigious of tombs. The tomb is all the more original in that it highlights one of the most important specific characteristics of Roland's tale. The entire *Chanson* bathes in nature, a mountainous setting in which the hero's epic is constantly unfolding under an open sky. It is remarkable that the legendary memory of Roland is often shown in nature. It is in nature that he left his essential mythical traces, such as rocks like those cut in two by Durandal (for example, Roland's Breach, close to the Cirque de Gavarnie in the French Pyrenees, or in Italy at the 'scoglio di Orlando', Roland's Rock, in San Terenzo, near La Spezia). Many places, notably in Italy, also bear the mark of Roland's 'knees'. As we have seen, a hero is linked to a place, a space; Roland is a multi-spatial hero.

Roland has also been inserted in the imaginary world of another type of marvellous man, the giant. On the slopes of Ronco di Maglio, near Savona, he has left the trace of a gigantic foot, known in the local dialect as the 'zampa du Ruland'. Perhaps the most unlikely image of the hero is the stone statue, five metres high, that was erected in 1404 in front of the Rathaus at Bremen, Germany, to replace a wooden statue that had been burned down. It still stands there as a symbol of the rights and privileges of the city.

During the period generally considered to be a transition from the Middle Ages to the Renaissance, although for me it is just one phase in the historical Middle Ages that continued until the eighteenth century, Roland underwent an important metamorphosis. In Italy he was appropriated by an ideological and cultural movement headed by the Este family in Ferrara. There, Roland became the hero of new tales overflowing with the chivalrous spirit, becoming one of the most wonderful products of the flamboyant medieval imaginary. The works that present this new image of Roland were created by two great writers favoured by the Este princes. The humanist Matteo Maria Boiardo composed his *Orlando innamorato* between 1476 and 1494, combining the Carolingian cycle and the Arthurian romance. His particular contribution was to develop convoluted amorous subplots, in particular one involving Roland and a new love, the beautiful Angelica. Boiardo inspired Ludovico Ariosto, a later court poet at Ferrara, to compose his *Orlando furioso* (1515–32). The story recounts the war between the miscreant kings Agramant and Rodomont (from whose name comes the word 'rodomontade', meaning extravagant boasting) and the Christians Charlemagne and Roland. In it we see the ill-fated love of Roland and Angelica, which causes Roland to sink into madness, from which the poem takes its title. But we also see the love of the Saracen Roger for the female Christian knight Bradamante and his conversion to Christianity, which was said to be the origin of the House of Este. In Ariosto, Roland becomes the hero of a flamboyant medieval imaginary, a chivalrous and treasured hero. Roland's legacy sometimes remained close to the old *Chanson de Roland*, and was sometimes marked by the more modern *Orlando furioso*. In Sicily there developed a tradition of decorating the local donkey carts with scenes from Ariosto, both carved and painted. Above all the Opera dei Pupi, a Sicilian form of puppet theatre telling exuberant tales of Christians against Saracens, has helped keep the old stories alive. It was Ariosto's adoption of the term 'paladin' for a chivalrous hero in *Orlando furioso* that brought it into common use. The word comes from the French *palatin*, which in thirteenth-century Italian became *paladino*, a valorous figure, a knight and, in particular, one of Charlemagne's peers. The term returned to France in the sixteenth century via Ariosto, and henceforth Roland belonged to a specific type of chivalrous hero, the paladins.

Christian Amalvi has shown how another lineage within the history of the imaginary in nineteenth-century France gave birth to a national and even secular Roland. Like most of the heroes of the Middle Ages, Roland was embraced by Romanticism, and in France two great Romantic poets wrote poems about him that were recited by schoolchildren all over France by the end of the century: Alfred de Vigny's 'Le Cor' (1826) and Victor Hugo's collection *La Légende des siècles* (1859–83). Francisque Xavier Michel's edition of the *Chanson de Roland* (1837) was both scholarly and accessible. After Victor Duruy introduced the teaching of history in elementary schools in 1867, the *Chanson de Roland* would become a historical resource as soon as translations in modern French became available. The most influential of these was published by Léon Gautier in 1872, at a time when he was already working on his *La Chevalerie* (1884), which ensured he was immersed in the ideology of that class of medieval society.

After 1870 Roland took his place among the warrior heroes who were recruited by elementary and secondary school teachers under the banner of revenge for defeat in the Franco-Prussian War, such as Vercingetorix, Bertrand du Guesclin, Joan of Arc, the Chevalier de Bayard, the Viscount of Turenne, Lazare Hoche and François Séverin Marceau. The vanquished Roland was prominent among them, intended to inspire the Catholics and supporters of the exiled monarchy, which is understandable, but, more surprisingly, also Republicans and laymen. But Jules Michelet taught readers to consider the *Chanson de Roland* as a work reflecting the popular French genius, as an emanation of the collective soul. Joan of Arc, canonized after the First World War, and also recognized by French people of all ideologies, would take the place that Roland had had in the second half of the nineteenth century.

The hero Roland's place in the European imaginary is rather vague today. In Italy, in addition to the Sicilian puppets, there have been a few attempts to continue Ariosto's legacy in films such as *Orlando e i Paladini di Francia* (or *Roland, the Mighty*; dir. Pietro Francisci, 1958) and *I paladini* (or *Hearts and Armour*; dir. Giacomo Battiato, 1984); in France Roland seems to have inspired only one silent short, *Roland à Roncevaux* (1910), by the extraordinarily prolific Louis

Feuillade, who made more than sixty films in that year alone, and a very marginal, though fascinating, work, *La Chanson de Roland* (dir. Frank Cassenti, 1978).

Today, a renaissance of the hero Roland doesn't seem likely, although the widespread revival of operas by Handel, Vivaldi and other eighteenth-century composers, who regularly drew upon Ariosto for their plots, has made the names of his characters more recognizable. But the imaginary is so dependent on the vagaries and avatars of history that we can never know if the paladin who appeared in so many dreams will not rediscover a place in the European imaginary.

TRISTAN AND ISEULT

According to Jean-Marie Fritz, 'The legend of Tristan and Iseult, along with the Grail, is the greatest myth conceived by the medieval West, a myth of ill-fated love leading to death.'

If this legend has become a myth characteristic of the European imaginary, it has also often been connected either to universal folklore or to a legend of Persian origin, that of Vis and Ramin, which recalls the story of the trio Mark, Tristan and Iseult. The essence of the legend, however, seems to have come from Celtic culture and spread throughout Christian Europe from the twelfth century. What is more, though Tristan and Iseult are emblematic heroes from the Middle Ages, they are in no way confined to that era and have become the embodiment of modern love. Although the Grail, as a marvel of the Middle Ages, is mentioned here only in chapters presenting chivalrous heroes, Tristan and Iseult have a rightful place because, better than any other myth, they present the medieval image of a woman, as well as that of a couple, and of an emotion that, alongside feudal loyalty, was probably the greatest legacy of affective values bequeathed to the West by the Middle Ages: courtly love.[1]

The myth is found in a series of generally fragmented texts, notably two romances in verse. The first was written in England by Thomas of Britain in 1170–73 and is reckoned to be a 'courtly' version; only about a quarter of the text remains. The other, written around 1180 by Béroul, a poet of Norman origin, is called the common or 'vulgar' version; only a fragment of 4,485 verses survives. In addition there are three tales in verse: two *Folies de Tristan*, which have been named after the places where the manuscripts were discovered, the *Folie de Berne* and *Folie d'Oxford*; the third story is a lay by Marie de France, the *Lai du chèvrefeuille* (118 lines). There is also the Scandinavian saga of Tristan and Iseult, written by the monk Robert to a commission by King Haakon IV of Norway (1226). The *Tristan en prose* (*Prose Tristan*, *c.* 1230) is a rewriting of the myth of Tristan and Iseult in the form of a very long romance, influenced by the *Lancelot en prose*: the tale unfolds both in the court of King Mark, the husband of Iseult and the uncle of Tristan, and in that of King Arthur. Tristan becomes a knight of the Round Table, and a seeker of the Grail. Very early on, the myth of Tristan and Iseult spread throughout Christian Europe, and mention should be made of the romance *Tristant* by Eilhart von Oberge, from the last quarter of the twelfth century, and the adaptations, still in Middle High German, composed between 1200 and 1210 by Gottfried von Strassburg and his continuators, Ulrich von Türheim and Heinrich von Freiberg. Around 1300 an anonymous author wrote *Sir Tristrem* in Middle English. An Italian version in prose found in the Biblioteca Riccardiana in Florence can be dated to the end of the thirteenth century and has been called the *Tristano Riccardiano*.

Putting these texts together, it is possible to make a summary of the legend of Tristan and Iseult. The orphan Tristan was raised by his uncle, King Mark of Cornwall. During a voyage to Ireland, Tristan saves Iseult, the daughter of the queen of Ireland, from a dragon (here, there is a connection between the legend of St George and

Tristan drinks a love philtre in Tristan de Léonois, *Tristan et Iseult*, manuscript, 15th century.

Tristan's chivalrous character), and obtains her hand for King Mark. During the sea voyage back to England, however, they mistakenly drink the love potion Iseult's mother has prepared for her daughter and King Mark. Drawn to each other by an irresistible love, they become lovers. Iseult's maid, who was responsible for making the mistake over the potion, takes her mistress's place during her wedding night with King Mark, to whom she sacrifices her virginity. In a series of burlesque incidents, Tristan and Iseult seek to hide their love from the suspicious King Mark, his barons, who are hostile to the young couple, and his vassals, who have King Mark more or less at their mercy. Finally, caught in flagrante delicto, they are sentenced to death by King Mark. They flee into the Wood of Morois, where they are forced to wander in wretched conditions. When Mark finds them they are chastely contrite; he forgives them, and they return to court.

Iseult is pardoned from the accusation of adultery by taking an ambiguous oath. Tristan takes his revenge against his baron enemies, but King Mark exiles him. The lovers henceforth see each other only from time to time, in hiding, when Tristan comes to court disguised as a pilgrim, a jongleur or a madman. He marries the daughter of the king of Carhaix, Iseult of the White Hands, but remains faithful to Iseult (the Fair), and does not consummate his marriage to the other Iseult. Wounded by a poisoned arrow, he summons Iseult the Fair to his deathbed. But Iseult of the White Hands, who is jealous, instead of displaying the white veil that should announce Iseult the Fair's arrival, displays a black veil instead, announcing her absence. A distraught Tristan allows himself to die, and Iseult the Fair can only throw herself onto the dead body and die in turn.

The myth of Tristan and Iseult had a profound impression on the European imaginary. The image of the couple and of love in general have been highly influenced by it. The potion became the symbol of love at first sight and of the fatality of love. The story of the trio strongly associated passionate love with adultery. Finally, the myth enrooted in the Western imaginary the idea of a fatal connection between love and death. This appears as early as the thirteenth century, when Gottfried von Strassburg wrote:

> They may have died a long time ago, but their charming names continue to live, and their deaths will live for a long time to come, forever, for the good of this world; for us their deaths will continue to be alive and new . . . We will read of their

lives, we will read of their deaths, and they will be sweeter for us than bread.

We can also note the relative fading and powerlessness of Mark, both as a husband and a king. Tristan and Iseult are inscribed within the limitations of conjugal power and monarchical power. The myth situates love in marginality, if not in rebellion.

The question has been raised as to whether the myth of Tristan and Iseult comes entirely from the courtly world, or whether it escapes it at least partially. It indeed seems that even in the courtly version uncourtly aspects, which we will see in the ideology of the troubadours, mark the myth of Tristan and Iseult. Christiane Marchello-Nizia has stressed that the story is situated outside courtly ethics regarding relationships between a knight and his lady.

> The courtly lady first has this civilizing function; she integrates the young man into feudal society, makes him share its values … The story of Tristan, on the contrary, appears as a series of renunciations, as a progressive marginalization, leading to death. Within this perspective, we must examine Tristan's disguises: unlike the courtly lady who encourages the use of weapons, the love Tristan brings to Iseult inspires not his fighting abilities, but his wiles and invention.

The myth of Tristan and Iseult still enthralled the imaginaries of men and women in the fifteenth and sixteenth centuries: the English poet Thomas Malory composed a very popular *Tristram de Lyones*, for example, in the mid-fifteenth century, and Danish ballads were dedicated to the legend in the sixteenth. The German poet Hans Sachs wrote *Tristan mit Isolde* in 1553 and a *Tristan and*

Iseult appeared in Serbo-Croatian in 1580. After fading in the seventeenth and eighteenth centuries, the myth experienced the usual Romantic revival. August Schlegel failed to complete his version of the story in 1800, but Walter Scott published *Sir Tristrem* (1804) and an Icelandic saga of *Tristan* was published in 1831.

The revival and spread of the myth of Tristan and Iseult in nineteenth-century France were connected to works of scholarship. Francisque Xavier Michel produced the corpus of Tristan romances in verse from 1835 to 1839. A modern reconstruction of the Tristan corpus under the title *Le Roman de Tristan et Iseult* was published by Joseph Bédier in 1900, enabling what the author described as 'a beautiful story of love and death' to reach a wide audience.

In the meantime, Tristan and Iseult lived again in English poetry through Matthew Arnold's poem in three parts 'Tristram and Iseult' (1852), and Algernon Swinburne's *Tristram of Lyonesse* (1882). They experienced new life above all thanks to the music of Richard Wagner, who laid out an initial plan for *Tristan und Isolde* in 1854, accentuating the tragic and pessimistic nature of the myth under the influence of Schopenhauer. In August 1857 he set aside work on *Siegfried* to write the libretto in less than a month. Once he had secured a publishing deal in early 1858 he started to compose the score act by act, completing it in August 1859. Difficulties in securing the funding and a cast capable of singing the demanding work delayed the first performance until 1865 at the Hoftheater in Munich under the direction of Hans von Bülow, just as Wagner was beginning an affair with Cosima, Bülow's wife and Liszt's daughter. Their affair resulted in the birth of a daughter, Isolde, whom von Bülow accepted as his own.

In the twentieth century, after the opera in the nineteenth, it was film that would offer the myth of Tristan and Iseult a new masterpiece, one that infused new life into the fateful couple under the banner of love and death. The film is *L'Éternel Retour* (or *Love Eternal*; dir. Jean Delannoy, 1943), with a screenplay by Jean Cocteau. It is set in 1940s France and the mythical lovers are played by Jean Marais and Madeleine Sologne.

Two troubadours in a Spanish manuscript, 13th century.

TROUBADOURS
AND TROUVÈRES

'Troubadour' is the French version of the Old Provençal *trobador*, which appeared in the twelfth century. The term describes the lyrical poets who founded Languedoc literature and introduced in Europe what became known at the end of the nineteenth century as 'courtly love'. The term 'trouvère' is the *langue d'oil* version of *trobador*, and designates the *langue d'oil* poets, the counterparts of Occitan troubadours, who appeared a bit later in northern France. The term comes from the Occitan *trobar*, to find, and means an inventor of words and poems. The emphasis placed on the creative genius of the troubadour, his cultural and social role in Occitania and later in all of Christian Europe in the twelfth and thirteenth centuries, is such that the troubadour and the trouvère may indeed be considered among the heroes of the Middle Ages, and the literature they created, the values – essentially love – whose praises they sang are nothing short of marvels.

The literature of the troubadours was a secular creation developed in the feudal courts of southern Europe, first in Aquitaine and Provence, then in Catalonia and northern Italy. Troubadours are another example here of the multiple places and cultural origins that were the principal components of medieval culture. We have seen the importance of Celtic culture; the troubadours reflect the importance of the culture of Occitania.

Troubadours were the inventors and the cantors of *finámor*, which is partially associated with courtliness, the aristocratic ideal of the art of living that implied politesse, refinement of manners and elegance, but also a sense of chivalrous honour. *Finámor* was a love relationship that set in motion the art of loving as developed by the troubadours. The object of that relationship was a married woman, who inspired in a lover a feeling that he expressed while courting her, presenting her with a request in the form of a message expressed through the poems or songs of troubadours. Such a liaison was based on the feudal-vassal model: the beloved woman was the lady (*mi dona* means 'milord' in Occitan), and the male lover, as well as the troubadour who is his messenger, was her vassal.

The goal of *finámor* was the affective and carnal satisfaction that troubadours called *joy*. *Finámor* has been described as 'an erotic mastery of desire'. Despite its connection to courtliness, the poetry of the troubadours sometimes fell into anti-courtly currents. René Nelli asserts that there existed

> in all periods of Occitan lyrics, 'wild poems', that didn't conform to the courtly ideal, and were a reaction against it, in which the egoistic and misogynist instincts of those bawdy and fighting barons were given free rein, as crudely as in the songs of the ancient *goliards*. This has been called anti-conformist literature, discourtly love, obscene lyrics.

There is a question that is still being debated today: did the troubadours serve to promote and exalt women, or were they only the mouthpieces of a fundamental misogyny in medieval society?

Jean-Charles Huchet defines *finámor* as 'the art of putting a woman at a distance through words'. Servants of a lady, the troubadours would then also be their jailers. The figure of the troubadour and his literary and musical production have commonly been linked to an aristocratic centre, the court. More arguable, regarding the troubadours' patrons, is the role that has been attributed to a few women of the aristocracy. Though it is highly likely that Ermengarde, Viscountess of Narbonne (d. 1196) and, in northern France, the Countess Marie de Champagne (d. 1198), daughter of Louis VI of France, among others, were patrons of the great poet Chrétien de Troyes, the patronage of Eleanor of Aquitaine (1122–1204) is less certain.

The first recognized troubadour was a great lord, William IX, Duke of Aquitaine from 1086 to 1126, who made his capital, Poitiers, the centre where troubadours first flourished. But if William IX was a great lyricist, he was also an obscene and misogynist poet. In the middle of the thirteenth century, his *Vida* asserts: 'The count of Poitiers was one of the great deceivers of women. He knew the art of making verses and singing and wandering throughout the world to better seduce women.'

The art of the troubadours spread in northern France thanks to the trouvères, their heroic counterparts in the North. The regions where there were the most trouvères and where they were most active were Champagne, Picardy and the Artois. In the thirteenth century they spread throughout northern France, and the city of Arras, where bourgeois and trouvères met in a cultural society, the Puy d'Arras, became a great centre of lyrical poetry and music. The Occitan troubadour Jaufré Rudel, lord of Blaye, invented the poetry of *amor de lonh* (love from afar), which his *vida* associated with his death on a crusade, probably the Second Crusade of 1147. The troubadour Marcabru (*fl.* 1130–50) was the first poet of *trobar clus* poetry ('*trouver fermé*' or 'to find closed'), a hermetic form of troubadour poetry that charmed many Europeans, including the young Francis of Assisi.

In addition to love, war was also a favourite theme of the troubadours who sang of the prowess of warrior heroes. Thus, Bertran de Born (1159–1195) declares:

> I tell you, I never enjoy eating, drinking, and sleeping as much as I do hearing the shout: '*Sus!*' from both sides, hearing the dismounted horses whinnying and the shouting, 'help, help!' and seeing both the humble and the great fall onto the grass in ditches, and seeing, stuck in the sides of the dead, the glittering lances with their pennants.

The Albigensian Crusade (1209–29) shook the society that had created the troubadours and their work began to change, in particular because it came to be expressed in new literary genres, such as the romance. *Flamenca*, a romance composed in Rouergue within the entourage of the lord of Roquefeuille during the second half of the thirteenth century, is the story of a lord duped by his young wife and her lover. The biographies of the troubadours (*Vidas*) that were now being written turned these literary heroes into social heroes, as well. The *Vidas* included texts, *razos*, which explained the connections between the life of the troubadour and his work to the glory of *finámor*.

From the beginning the social status of the troubadours was quite diverse, bringing together great lords, low and middle-ranking nobles, bourgeois and vagabonds, all in the service of essentially aristocratic values. It is notable, however, that the number of non-noble troubadours increased during the thirteenth century, even if their production often continued to be stamped with the seal of courtliness.

Scholars believe that Guiraut Riquier (*c.* 1230–*c.* 1295), born in Narbonne of modest origins, was 'the last troubadour', working for Aimery IV, Viscount of Narbonne and Alfonso X of Castile. He was in any case the last great poet of *finámor*. The final novelty, at the end of the thirteenth century, was that troubadours increasingly sang the praises of an exceptional lady whose cult had attained extraordinary popularity: the Virgin Mary.

Even more clearly perhaps than for other heroes of the medieval imaginary, with Romanticism the troubadours again became cultural heroes, particularly in France. Furthermore, a revival of regional languages and passions brought the troubadours back to life at the centre of an Occitan renaissance. Gaston Paris used the expression 'courtly love' for the first time in an 1883 article on Chrétien de Troyes, but this was preceded by the use of 'troubadour style' since 1851 to describe a pseudo-Gothic style in architecture, and historians of literature had been talking about the 'troubadour genre' since 1876.

Today, troubadours are still heroes well integrated in the European imaginary and keenly present in Occitan memory. Troubadours have been adopted by most popular forms of contemporary culture, including the worlds of advertising and music. The Fabulous Trobadors, a duo from Toulouse who combine rap and beatbox, are a good example of this.

The unicorn in a French manuscript, *c.* 1480.

THE UNICORN

With the unicorn we enter the world of marvellous animals, one that held a very large place in the medieval imaginary, and is still important today in the European imaginary. The unicorn is a good example of the presence of imaginary beings among the heroes of the Middle Ages, and alongside historical figures or real animals. The destiny of the unicorn, as a heroic figure, illustrates on the one hand how indifferent the men and women of the Middle Ages for a long time were to any dividing line between the imaginary and reality, and, on the other, their passion for unusual, highly symbolic heroes.

The unicorn was bequeathed to the Middle Ages by antiquity. The Church Fathers, Christian authors from the High Middle Ages, found the creature in a work that is the source of the animal's formidable presence in Western medieval culture: the *Physiologus*, a treatise written in Greek in Alexandria between the second and fourth century in a probably Gnostic setting. It is imbued with symbolic religiosity and was very soon translated into Latin. The unicorn's success has been attributed to its aesthetic qualities, and above all to its close connection with Christ and the Virgin within medieval religious sensibility. The unicorn is cited three times by Pliny in his *Natural History* (8, 31, 76) and by Gaius Julius Solinus, a third-century grammarian, who provided the Middle Ages with its largest stock of marvels in his *Collectanea rerum memorabilium* (Collection of Curiosities). But the decisive text remains the *Physiologus*:

> He is a small animal like the kid, is exceedingly shrewd, and has one horn in the middle of his head. The hunter cannot approach him because he is extremely strong. How then do they hunt the beast? Hunters place a chaste virgin before him. He bounds forth into her lap and she warms and nourishes the animal and takes him into the palace of kings.[1]

The introduction of the unicorn into the pseudo-scientific and symbolic canon of the Middle Ages can be seen further in several fundamental texts: Gregory the Great's *Moralia in Job* (31, 15), Isidore of Seville's *Etymologies* (12, 2, 12–13), the Venerable Bede's *Commentaries on the Psalms* (Psalm 77) and Rabanus Maurus' encyclopedia *De rerum naturis* (On the Nature of Things) (VIII.1). The success of the unicorn in the twelfth century can be seen by its presence in the very popular poems of the *Carmina Burana*. But above all, the unicorn became an important character in the *Bestiaries*, those collections of half-scientific, half-fictional and always moralizing texts that brought together real animals and imaginary animals within the same belief system using their power of attraction.

The common description of the unicorn is borrowed from the *Physiologus*. The unicorn is a ferocious animal and kills with its horn any hunter who comes close; but if it encounters a virgin, the animal leaps on her breast and the girl nurses it and then captures it. The virginity of the girl is the indispensable condition for the success of the hunt.

The unicorn, like all legacies from antiquity, underwent a process of Christianization in the Middle Ages. It was an image of the Saviour; it became a horn of salvation and found its home at the breast of the Virgin Mary. It became an illustration of the Gospel text, 'And the Word was made flesh and dwelt among us' (John 1:14). The unicorn is related to the quintessential virgin, Mary; the act of hunting it represented allegorically the mystery of the Incarnation in which the unicorn itself represented the one-horned spiritual Christ (*Christus spiritualis unicornis*), and its horn became the cross of Christ. And so, through its identification both with the Virgin Mary and with Jesus Christ, the unicorn was at the centre of Christian symbolism, and that dual identification has enabled some historians, by leaning on the dual symbolism of the medieval unicorn, to insist on the androgynous nature of Christianity. Thus the unicorn would have bequeathed to the European imaginary an image of a bisexual human model.

The poem *De la licorne* (Of the Unicorn), taken from the *Bestiaire divin*, the longest bestiary in French verse, written around 1210–11 by William the Clerk of Normandy, is a good example of this belief.

> We will speak to you of the unicorn:
> it is an animal that has only one horn,
> placed right in the middle of its forehead.
> This beast is so fierce,
> So aggressive and so bold
> that it attacks the elephant,
> the most formidable of animals
> that exist in the world.
> The unicorn has a hoof that is so hard and sharp
> that it easily fights the elephant,

And the edge of its hoof is so sharp
that nothing is struck by it
without being stabbed or torn.
The elephant doesn't have the strength to defend itself
when it attacks,
because it strikes under its belly so strongly,
with its hoof that slices like a blade,
that it completely disembowels the elephant.
This beast is so strong
that it fears no hunter.
Those who want to try
to catch it through trickery and to tie it down,
when it has gone off to have fun
in the mountains or a valley,
once they have discovered its lair
and have tracked it carefully,
they go get a damsel
whom they know is a virgin;
then they have her sit down and wait
at the animal's den to capture it.
When the unicorn has arrived
and seen the young girl,
it goes straight to her
and lays down on her lap;
then the hunters who were watching spring out;
they seize it and tie it down,
then they bring it before the king
by force and impetuosity.
This extraordinary beast
which has only one horn on its head,

represents Our Lord
Jesus Christ, our Saviour.
It is the celestial unicorn,
which resides on the breast of the Virgin,
which is so worthy of veneration;
in it, he takes a human form
and thus appears to the eyes of the world;
his people don't recognize him.
On the contrary, the Jews watch for him
and ultimately grab him and tie him down;
they take him before Pilate,
and there, they sentence him to death.

The end of the poem shows how the imaginary was used in the Middle Ages to enflame and justify the most condemnable passions. Here, the unicorn is enlisted by anti-Judaism, the ancestor of anti-Semitism.

However, the theme of the unicorn had a tendency to be watered down during the Middle Ages and to appear above all in the marvellous landscape of love. Thus Count Thibaut IV of Champagne (1201–1253), a famous troubadour, presents himself in his poems as the perfect lover of the great courtly song. In one of his most famous poems, he identifies with the unicorn:

I am like the unicorn
troubled at seeing
the young girl who enchants it,
so joyful at its plight
that overwhelmed it falls on her lap,
and that then is killed out of treason.

I, too, have been killed, in the same way,
by love and my Lady, yes, it's true:
they have my heart which I cannot take back.

One of the most interesting attempts to find a place for the unicorn in the world of real animals is that of the great theologian Albertus Magnus, whose treatise *De animalibus* (On Animals) is the most remarkable medieval study of animals. He describes the unicorn as an animal with one horn: a monoceros fish, which could only be the narwhal, or the rhinoceros that lives in the mountains and deserts. But myth caught up with Albertus. According to him, the rhinoceros 'adores young virgins and upon seeing them he approaches them and falls asleep next to them'. The unicorn succeeded in seducing the theologian.

The medieval unicorn was not content simply to feed the imaginaries of the Christians in the Middle Ages. It could also be of great benefit to them. As with many medieval marvels, the unicorn travelled between the imaginary world and the real world. The belief in its existence pushed the people of the Middle Ages to look for it in an existing animal. They thought they could identify it with one or other of these animals: the narwhal or the rhinoceros. The identification obviously came from the existence of only one horn on both of those animals, but the narwhal's horn was only material, whereas that of the rhinoceros was symbolic, because in the allegorical world of the Middle Ages the rhinoceros was one of the incarnations of Christ.

But what was the unicorn's horn used for? It was believed to be a powerful antidote against poison, a danger that haunted the men and women of the Middle Ages, and which was indeed practised widely at that time. Unicorn horn could be an antidote and prevent its effects, which is why it was sought, especially by important figures, and this also explains its presence in church and royal treasuries. The horns that have been preserved up to the present are generally narwhal horns. Among the most famous of these so-called unicorn horns is the narwhal tusk (1.6 metres long) recorded in the treasury of the abbey of Saint-Denis in the late fifteenth century and now in the Musée de Cluny, Paris. One of the two narwhal tusks in the treasury of San Marco, Venice, has a carved inscription in Greek on how the unicorn offers protection against poisons.

The unicorn horn of Saint-Denis appears in the inventory made for King Francis II (r. 1559–60). Article 1 of the inventory describes it like this:

> A large unicorn horn starting from the tip, embellished with gold and standing on its base on three unicorn heads made of gold, the said unicorn horn weighing only 17 *marcs* 1 ounce and a half, and with a length of 5 feet 3 inches, and this does not include a little decoration at the tip, which with the other decoration of the said three unicorn heads together weigh 23 *marcs* and a half, estimated at 1,504 *écus*.

Jean Bodin was less prosaic in his *Universae naturae theatrum* (1596):

> I dare not assert here from which of those two beasts, monoceros or unicorn, is the horn that is seen in Saint-Denis in France; all the same, it is more than 6 feet long, being so hollow, that it could hold more than a quart of liquor; it is attributed with having admirable power against venom; the common man calls it a unicorn.

Its virtues could be accessed by touching it, but access to the horns was limited to the rich and powerful; common people could find it on the market in the form of unicorn powder. The demand was abundant, but there was ample supply.[2]

In the fifteenth century the unicorn inspired one of the most famous and beautiful works of art, which even today assures the animal a choice place in the human imaginary. It is the tapestry series *The Lady and the Unicorn* (Musée de Cluny, Paris), acquired in 1882 after long negotiations with the municipality of Boussac, Creuse, where the series had been in the château for nearly two hundred years. Edmond Du Sommerard, in his 1883 catalogue, added in an appendix: 'The most prestigious acquisition of his career, which became the most famous work in the Cluny museum.' The set of six tapestries represent the five senses. The unicorn appears in the allegorical tapestry of 'touch' in which the Lady lays her hand on the unicorn's horn, and in that of 'sight' in which the Lady holds up a mirror that reflects the image of the unicorn. But the essential role of the unicorn in this grouping is to hold pennants that bear the motto '*A mon seul désir*'.

The reference that emerges out of these symbolic images is essentially concerned with love. The spirit of that work of art has been associated with the sermons of the great theologian Jean Gerson (1363–1429). Gerson defines a sixth sense in the work, that of the heart or understanding, which traces a path leading to God. These ideas, which are found among the Neoplatonic humanists such as the Florentine Marsilio Ficino, spread throughout France at the end of the fifteenth century. Critics have also seen in these tapestries an allegory of marriage, as the tapestry must have been commissioned by a member of the great Le Viste family from Lyon at the very end of the fifteenth century, perhaps on the occasion of a marriage. In any event, as regards the art of the tapestry, it encompasses allegorical thinking and a presentation of the unicorn, and is an expression of seigneurial tastes at the turn of the sixteenth century. One finds the theme of the unicorn again in other tapestries of the time, in particular in the *Hunt of the Unicorn* series (*c.* 1500) exhibited in the Cloisters museum in New York. One may conclude along with Fabienne Joubert:

> The tapestry belongs to those artistic realms in which the phenomenon of fashion played an essential role, and it is therefore logical to find in *The Lady and the Unicorn* the spiritual and artistic preoccupations of the time combined with a concern on the part of the one who commissioned it with asserting his power through heraldry.

The 'fashion' of the unicorn, as we have seen, continued through the sixteenth century. It combined a taste for the beauty of forms with a scientific search for a real marvel and the quest for antidotal or spiritual virtues. The engraver, goldsmith and medal-maker Jean Duvet devoted a large portion of his œuvre to the unicorn. The goldsmith of Francis I and Henry II, he engraved, among other things, the plates for the illustrations in *L'Histoire de la licorne* (*c.* 1520), and so earned the name of the Master of the Unicorn. This interest in unicorns, which fell between science and myth, seems to have continued into the seventeenth century, since the inventory of art belonging to Cardinal Mazarin contains the following mention in 1661: 'A unicorn horn 7 feet long or about with a Moroccan case from the Levant, red with gold threads, taken together 2 *marcs.*'

In the nineteenth century the unicorn underwent the usual renaissance experienced by the medieval imaginary. It reappeared above all in symbolist painting, inspiring true masterpieces by Gustave Moreau, Arnold Böcklin and Arthur B. Davies. If, as a gift from the Middle Ages, the unicorn settled into the Western imaginary, its status is probably due to the elegance of its shape and the wealth of its symbolic potentiality, thanks to which it has been found in Gnosticism, alchemy, Judaism and Eastern traditions. In the West, the unicorn seems to have survived mainly as an emblem. It is the logo of a retail company, the name of a boat in the *Tintin* comics, and the logo of Amiens SC football club (the team are called Les Licornes). But the unicorn, probably more than the other marvels of the Middle Ages, must await further resurrections.

In 1993 the great Danish sculptor Jørn Ronnau created two beautiful sculptures of unicorn horns. He declared that he was interested in the unicorn as a 'superb metaphor of the universal mystery of nature'. And he gave as a source for his inspiration the treatises of alchemists 'on the nature of deep knowledge'. The Christian Middle Ages thus does not have a monopoly over the European imaginary.

THE VALKYRIE

'Valkyrie' comes from two Old Norse words meaning 'fallen' and 'to choose'. Valkyries appear to have been early demons of the dead or psychopomp demons in Scandinavian mythology, escorting souls to the afterlife.

During the time of the Vikings, Valkyries seem to have transformed either into Amazons or into the daughters of Odin, the principal Scandinavian god. They are virgins who lead warriors who have died heroically on the battlefield to Walhalla, the primitive Scandinavian paradise. We find traces of the Valkyries in the *Nibelungenlied* and other Germanic epics that were set down in verse or prose from the end of the twelfth century, drawing upon legends and songs that had long been spread orally. The main texts are the *Poetic Edda*, songs of gods and heroes composed between the ninth and twelfth centuries and contained in an Icelandic manuscript from the last third of the thirteenth century, the *Prose Edda* attributed to the Icelandic poet Snorri Sturluson (1179–1241), and the *Völsunga saga* (late thirteenth century), which connects the lineage of the Völsung clan, ancestors of Sigurd, with Odin, the main god of Germanic mythology.

An imaginary heroine, the Valkyrie appears here because she embodies the important presence alongside Celtic influences of

Scandinavian and Germanic imaginaries within that of the Middle Ages, as bequeathed to the European imaginary. Like Tristan and Iseult, the Valkyrie also asserts the historical importance of the legacy of the medieval imaginary through the work of Richard Wagner in the nineteenth century.

There were generally nine, sometimes twelve, Valkyries. The Valkyrie, who became a heroine of the medieval Germanic epic from the end of the twelfth century, embodied the character Brunhild (Brynhildr) in the *Nibelungenlied*. Brunhild disobeys Odin, and he punishes her by making her sleep and taking away her status as a Valkyrie. Henceforth, she would be a mere mortal who would have to marry the one who awakens her; but she swears that she will marry only a man who has no fear. Brunhild is awakened by King Sigurd and they exchange vows without consummating their marriage. Brunhild then marries Gunnar (or Gunther), a Nibelung, while Sigurd marries Gudrun (or Kriemhild), Gunnar's sister. Brunhild is jealous and her honour has been wounded. She demands that Gunnar kill Sigurd, but it is Gutthorn, a third Nibelung, who kills Sigurd while he is sleeping. Brunhild, destroyed by her grief, immolates herself on the funerary pyre while Sigurd's body is burning.

The myth of the Valkyrie is another tale of the union of a supernatural being and a mortal, who is usually a knight or nobleman. The Valkyrie who became a mortal did not escape her supernatural origin. This heroine also illustrates the importance in the medieval imaginary of the violence of war and the fight against monsters: the woman is a being connected to death.

The Valkyrie, whose original role was to lead war heroes to paradise, in the end leads them into a love whose inevitable end is death. In Wagner's opera, the Valkyrie Brünnhilde is the favourite of the nine daughters of the supreme god Odin (here called Wotan). She

Poster for a French production of Richard Wagner's *The Valkyrie*, 1893.

is also his confidante. Brünnhilde disobeys her father and tries to protect Siegmund and his twin sister Sieglinde, who are the children of Wotan by a Völsung woman. Brünnhilde is condemned to sleep surrounded by fire until she is awoken by a hero who has no fear. This turns out to be Siegfried, the result of the incestuous union of Siegmund and Sieglinde. Siegfried, however, has been tricked by Gunther into securing Brünnhilde, who is now mortal, as his own bride. Brünnhilde joins the plot to murder Siegfried for his perfidy, but chooses to follow him into death on his funeral pyre. This act also sets fire to Valhalla, destroying the traditional divine universe. This *Götterdämmerung* (Twilight of the Gods), as Wagner called the fourth opera of his cycle, obviously evokes the twilight of Arthur and the Knights of the Round Table in *La Mort le roi Artu* from the beginning of the thirteenth century. The medieval imaginary is definitively placed under the banner of death, but also of renewal, and rests on connections and metamorphoses between the supernatural and the human worlds.

A revival of these half-divine, half-human heroes, including the Valkyrie, occurred in the twentieth century in film, in Fritz Lang's 1924 silent masterpiece *Die Nibelungen*, which is divided into two parts: *Siegfried* and *Kriemhild's Revenge*.

REFERENCES

INTRODUCTION

1 Évelyne Patlagean, 'L'histoire de l'imaginaire', in *La Nouvelle Histoire*, ed. Jacques Le Goff (Brussels, 1988), p. 307.

2 Jacques Le Goff, *L'Imaginaire médiéval* (Paris, 1985); as *The Medieval Imagination*, trans. Arthur Goldhammer (Chicago, IL, 1988).

3 On images and the historian, see Jean-Claude Schmitt, 'Images', in *Dictionnaire raisonné de l'Occident médiéval*, ed. Jacques Le Goff and Jean-Claude Schmitt (Paris, 1999), pp. 497–511; Jérôme Baschet and Jean-Claude Schmitt, eds, *L'Image: Fonctions et usages des images dans l'Occident médiéval*, Cahiers du Léopard d'or 5 (Paris, 1996); Jacques Le Goff, *Un Moyen Âge en images* (Paris, 2000); Jean Wirth, *L'Image médiévale: Naissance et développement (XIe–XVe siècle)* (Paris, 1989). On the symbolic, see the superb work by Michel Pastoureau, *Une histoire symbolique du Moyen Âge occidental* (Paris, 2003).

4 Jean-Claude Schmitt, 'Images', in *Dictionnaire raisonné de l'Occident médiéval*, ed. Le Goff and Schmitt, p. 499.

5 Jacques Le Goff, *Héros du Moyen Âge: le saint et le roi* (Paris, 2004).

6 The title of Duby's book is *Mâle moyen âge* (Paris, 1988). The English-language edition is *Love and Marriage in the Middle Ages* (Chicago, IL, 1994).

7 Robert Delort, 'Animaux', in *Dictionnaire raisonné de l'Occident médiéval*, ed. Le Goff and Schmitt, pp. 55–66.

8 Claude Lecouteux, *Les Monstres dans la pensée médiévale européenne* (Paris, 1993); J. B. Friedman, *The Monstrous Races in Mediaeval Art and Thought* (Cambridge, MA, and London, 1981).

9 *De l'étranger à l'étrange ou la 'conjointure' de la Merveille*, Senesciences
   25 (Aix-en-Provence, 1988); *Démons et merveilles au Moyen Âge: actes
   du IVe Colloque international* (Nice, 1990); Gervase of Tilbury,
   Le Livre des merveilles, trans. and ed. Annie Duchesne (Paris, 1992);
   Claude-Claire Kappler, *Monstres, démons et merveilles à la fin du
   Moyen Âge*, 2nd edn (Paris, 1999); Claude Lecouteux, 'Paganisme,
   christianisme et merveilleux', *Annales ESC*, XXXVII/4 (1982),
   pp. 700–716; Jacques Le Goff, 'Merveilleux', in *Dictionnaire
   raisonné de l'Occident médiéval*, ed. Le Goff and Schmitt,
   pp. 709–24; Michel Meslin, ed., *Le Merveilleux, l'imaginaire et les
   croyances en Occident* (Paris, 1984); Jacques Le Goff, 'Le merveilleux
   dans l'Occident médiéval', in *L'Imaginaire médiéval*, pp. 17–39; Daniel
   Poirion, *Le Merveilleux dans la littérature française au Moyen Âge*
   (Paris, 1982); Francis Dubost, 'Merveilleux', in *Dictionnaire du
   Moyen Âge*, ed. Cl. Gauvard, A. de Libera and M. Zink (Paris, 2002),
   pp. 906–10.

10 Rudolf Wittkower, 'Marvels of the East: A Study in the History of
   Monsters', *Journal of the Warburg and Courtauld Institutes*, V (1942),
   pp. 159–97; Lev Nikolaevich Gumilev, *Searches for an Imaginary
   Kingdom: The Legend of the Kingdom of Prester John* [1970]
   (Cambridge, 1987); C. Julius Solinus, *Collectanea rerum memorabilium*
   (Berlin, 1895); M. R. James, ed., *Marvels of the East: A Full
   Reproduction in Facsimile of the Three Known Copies of the Tractatus
   de diuresis monstrisquae sunt in mundo* (Oxford, 1929); Marco Polo,
   La Description du monde (Le Livre des merveilles), ed., trans. and
   intro. Pierre-Yves Badel (Paris, 1998); Pierre d'Ailly, 'De mirabilibus
   Indiae', *Imago mundi*, ed. E. Buron (Paris, 1930), pp. 264ff; *La lettera
   del Prete Gianni*, ed. Gioia Zaganelli (Parma, 1990); Gioia Zaganelli,
   L'Oriente incognito medieval (Saveria Manelli, 1997); Jacques Le Goff,
   'L'Occident médiéval et l'océan Indien: un horizon onirique', in *Pour
   un autre Moyen Âge* (Paris, 1977), pp. 280–306.

11 The moment of the twelfth–thirteenth centuries. Cf. Jacques Le Goff,
   'Naissance du roman historique du XIIe siècle?', *Le Roman historique*,
   special issue of *Nouvelle revue Française*, 238 (1972), pp. 163–73;
   Le Goff, 'Du ciel sur la terre: la mutation des valeurs du XIIe au XIIIe
   siècle dans l'Occident chrétien', in *Héros du Moyen Âge*, pp. 1263–87.

12 (Paris, 2003); Eng. trans. by Janet Lloyd as *The Birth of Europe* (Oxford, 2005).

13 For the posterity of the Middle Ages see Christian Amalvi, 'Moyen Âge', in *Dictionnaire raisonné de l'Occident médiéval*, ed. Le Goff and Schmitt, pp. 790–805; Christian Amalvi, *Le Goût du Moyen Âge* (Paris, 1996); Vittore Branca, ed., *Concetto, storia, miti e immagiti del medioevo* (Florence, 1973); Umberto Eco, 'Dieci modi di ignare il medioevo', in *Sugli specchi e altri saggi* (Milan, 1985), pp. 78–89; Horst Fuhrmann, *Überall ist Mittelalter: Von der Gegenwart einer vergangenen Zeit* (Munich, 1996); Jacques Le Goff and Guy Lobrichon, eds, *Le Moyen Âge aujourd'hui: Trois regards contemporains sur le Moyen Âge: histoire, théologie, cinema: Actes de la Rencontre de Cerisy-la-Salle, 1991* (Paris, 1998); Alain Boureau, 'Moyen Âge', in *Dictionnaire du Moyen Âge*, ed. Gauvard, de Libera and Zink, pp. 950–55.

14 For the Middle Ages and film, see Stuart Airlie, 'Strange Eventful Histories: The Middle Ages in the Cinema', in *The Medieval World*, ed Peter Linehan and Janet L. Nelson (London and New York, 2001), pp. 163–83; François de la Bretèque, 'Le regard du cinéma sur le Moyen Âge', in *Le Moyen Âge aujourd'hui*, ed. Le Goff and Lobrichon, pp. 283–326; *Le Moyen Âge au cinéma*, special issue of *Cahiers de la Cinémathèque*, 42–3 (1985); *Le Moyen Âge vu par le cinéma européen*, Cahiers de Conques 3 (2001). The postage stamp is also a modern support for the expression of the traditional imaginary.

ARTHUR

1 Cedric E. Pickford, 'Camelot', in *Mélanges de langue et de littérature médiévales offerts à Pierre Le Gentil* (Paris, 1973), pp. 633–40.

2 The great Italian historian of popular literature and folklore, Arturo Graf (1848–1913), devoted a wonderful article to 'Artú nell'Etna' in his *Miti, leggende e superstizioni del medioevo*, 2 vols (Turin, 1892–3), II, pp. 303–25; ed. Clara Allasia and Walter Meliga (Milan, 2002).

THE CASTLE

1 Jean-Marie Pesez, 'Château', in *Dictionnaire raisonné de l'Occident médiéval*, ed. Jacques Le Goff and Jean-Claude Schmitt (Paris, 1999), pp. 179–98.

2 Pierre Bonnassie, 'Château', in *Les cinquantes mots clefs de l'histoire médiévale* (Toulouse, 1981), p. 42.

3 The *braie* was a massive construction built in front of a fortified wall to make it stronger.

4 Pesez, 'Château'.

5 Jean-Paul Schneider, 'Un colosse au pied d'argile: le château vu par les dictionnaires du XVIIIe siècle', in *La Vie de château*, ed. F. X. Cuche (Strasbourg, 1998), pp. 33–43.

6 See Roland Recht, *Le Rhin* (Paris, 2001), p. 264.

7 Teresa of Avila in the sixteenth century had used the metaphor to evoke the spiritual life.

THE CATHEDRAL

1 See Roland Recht, 'L'objet de l'histoire de l'art', inaugural lecture at the Collège de France, 14 March 2002.

2 This was unfortunately lost in either title under which the English translation has been published, *The Cathedral Builders of the Middle Ages* (New York, 1993) and *Cathedrals and Castles: Building in the Middle Ages* (New York, 1995).

3 *Le temps des cathédrales*, written and narrated by Georges Duby, 6 parts, Antenne 2, 1978, www.youtube.com, accessed 7 August 2019.

4 James S. Ackerman, '"Ars sine scientia nihil est": Gothic Theory of Architecture at the Cathedral of Milan', *Art Bulletin*, XXXI/2 (1949), pp. 84–111.

5 Translation by A. S. Kline, see www.poetryintranslation.com/ PITBR/French/Verlaine.php.

CHARLEMAGNE

1 Eginhard [Einhard], *Early Lives of Charlemagne*, trans. A. J. Grant (London, 1900), available at www.yorku.ca/inpar/eginhard_grant.pdf, accessed 7 August 2019.
2 Elizabeth Artemis Clark, 'The Chronicle of Novalese: Translation, Text and Literary Analysis', PhD diss., University of North Carolina, 2017, pp. 73–4.
3 Chateaubriand, struck by the Romantic image offered by this imperial corpse sitting up, used the description in *Mémoires d'outre-tombe*, ed. Maurice Levaillant [1849–50] (Paris, 1948), I, pp. 316–17. He connects this discovery of a corpse sitting up on its throne to an imaginary exhumation of around 1450.
4 English translation in Maureen C. Miller, *Power and the Holy in the Age of the Investiture Conflict: A Brief History with Documents* (New York and Basingstoke, 2005), pp. 164–5.
5 There is, however, the film by Jean-François Delassus, *Au temps de Charlemagne* (Point du Jour pour Arte, 2003), for which the author was historical adviser. This attempts to restore the Carolingian civilization and the figure of Charlemagne into the history of civilizations.

KNIGHTS AND CHIVALRY

1 Pierre Bonnassie, *Les cinquantes mots clefs de l'histoire médiévale* (Toulouse, 1981), pp. 43–4.
2 Dominique Barthélemy, *Chevaliers et Miracles. La violence et le sacré dans la société féodale* (Paris, 2004).
3 Georges Duby, *William Marshal: The Flower of Chivalry*, trans. Richard Howard (New York, 1985), p. 152.
4 *Le Séminaire, livre xx, Encore* (Paris, 1975), p. 79.
5 *Tirant le Blanc*, trans. Jean-Marie Barberà (Toulouse, 2003), pp. 7–8.

THE LAND OF COCKAIGNE

1 *Journal d'un bourgeois de Paris,* ed. and intro. Colette Beaune (Paris, 1990), pp. 221–2. The *toise* was approximately the equivalent of 1.949m. The entertainment was presented as a new invention, but the name 'Cockaigne' was not mentioned.

MELUSINA

1 To date this has appeared in at least seven editions. See Pierre Brunel, 'Mélusine dans *Arcane 17* d'André Breton', in *Mélusines continentales et insulaires,* ed. Jeanne-Marie Boivin and Proinsias MacCana (Paris, 1999), pp. 327–42.
2 See the interesting chapter by Anita Guerreau-Jalabert, 'Des fées et des diables: Observations sur le sens des récits "mélusiniens" au Moyen Âge', in *Mélusines continentales et insulaires,* pp. 105–37.

POPE JOAN

1 Hilário Franco Júnior, *Cocanha: A Historia de une pais imaginário* (São Paulo, 1998); Fr. trans. as *Cocagne: Histoire d'un pays imaginaire,* preface by Jacques Le Goff (Paris, 2013).
2 Herbert Thurston, *Pope Joan* (London, 1917), p. 6.
3 'Je vous le gripperay au croc et sçavez que luy feray? Cor bleu! Je vous luy coupperay les couillons, tout rasibus du cul. Il ne s'en faudra un pelet [a hair] par ceste raison ne sera il jamais Pape car "testiculos non habet". *The Works of Rabelais,* trans. Sir Thomas Urquhart of Cromarty and Peter Antony Motteux [1693] (Derby, 1894), Book III, chap. 12, available at www.gutenberg.org.

REYNARD

1 Marcel Détienne and Jean-Pierre Vernant, *Les Ruses de l'intelligence: La 'métis' des Grecs* (Paris, 1974). See Jacques Le Goff, 'Reynard et la *métis* médiévale', in *Le Rire de Goupil, Renard, prince de l'entre-deux,* ed. Claude Rivals (Toulouse, 1998), pp. 95–103.

2 Buffon's text can be found in *Le Rire de Goupil*, ed. Rivals, pp. 185–9.

3 Reineke-Fuchs-Museum, Dresdener Strasse 22, 35440 Linden-Leihgestern, Germany.

4 See Marcelle Enderle, 'Le renard des albums pour enfants', in *Le Rire de Goupil*, ed. Rivals, pp. 319–26.

5 François de la Bretèque, 'Reynard au cinéma, un rendezvous manqué', in *Le Rire de Goupil*, ed. Rivals, pp. 327–35. I don't agree with the negative assessment by the excellent film historian François de la Bretèque. Reynard was metamorphosed in film, but he experienced a strong revival through it.

ROBIN HOOD

1 Langland writes: 'I know some ballads about Robin Hood and Randolph, Earl of Chester', *Piers Plowman: A New Translation of the B-text*, trans. A.V.C. Schmidt (Oxford, 1992), p. 55. Randulph de Blundevill, Earl of Chester (1172–1232), a historical figure, was also a popular hero who rose up against taxation. See R. H. Hilton, ed., *Peasants, Knight and Heretics* (Cambridge, 1976).

2 See Michel Pastoureau, 'Ivanhoé, un Moyen Âge exemplaire', in *Le Moyen Âge à livres ouverts: actes du Colloque, Lyon, 2002* (Paris, 2003), pp. 15–24; repr. as 'Le Moyen Âge d'Ivanhoé, un best-seller à l'époque romantique', in *Une histoire symbolique du Moyen Âge occidental* (Paris, 2004), pp. 327–38.

3 Walter Scott, *Ivanhoe: A Romance* (Edinburgh, 1863), p. 302.

4 The DVD and Blu-ray reissues of this film (2003 and 2008) include two Looney Tunes cartoons, *Rabbit Hood* (1949), in which the hero is Bugs Bunny (with a cameo appearance by Errol Flynn), and *Robin Hood Daffy* (1958), starring Daffy Duck with Porky Pig as Friar Tuck.

ROLAND

1 Jean Dufournet, *Cours sur la Chanson de Roland* (Paris, 1972).

2 Ibid.

TRISTAN AND ISEULT

1 Lancelot and Guinevere perhaps embody courtly love better than Tristan and Iseult. In the latter story the tragic fate of love is dominant, whereas the quintessence of courtly love is the *fin'amor* and *joy*. See Danielle Régnier-Bohler, 'Amour courtois', in *Dictionnaire raisonné de l'Occident médiéval*, ed. Jacques Le Goff and Jean-Claude Schmitt (Paris, 1999), pp. 32–41.

THE UNICORN

1 *Physiologus: A Medieval Book of Nature Lore*, trans. Michael J. Curley (Chicago, IL, 1979), p. 51.

2 I wish to thank Françoise Piponnier for informing me of these texts on unicorn powder published in Victor Gay and Henri Stern, 'Licorne', in *Glossaire archéologique du Moyen Âge et de la Renaissance*, 2 vols (Paris, 1885), II, pp. 76–8.

BIBLIOGRAPHY

INTRODUCTION

Jonin, Pierre, *L'Europe en vers au Moyen Âge : Essai de thématique* (Paris,
    1996): chivalry, pp. 351–69; jongleur, pp. 529–40; marvels, pp. 582–93
Le Goff, Jacques, *L'Imaginaire medieval* (Paris, 1985); as *The Medieval
    Imagination*, trans. Arthur Goldhammer (Chicago, IL, 1988)

ARTHUR

Arthurus rex: Acta conventus Lovaniensis, ed. W. Van Hoecke, G. Tourny
    and W. Verbeke (Leuven, 1991)
*Arthurus rex: Koning Arthur en Nederlanden: La Matière de Bretagne
    et les anciens Pays-Bas*, exh. cat., Leuven, Stedelijk Museum Vander
    Kelen-Mertens (1987).
La Légende arthurienne: Le Graal et la Table ronde, preface by Danielle
    Régnier-Bohler (Paris, 1989)
Barber, Richard, *King Arthur: Hero and Legend* (Woodbridge, 1993)
Boutet, Dominique, *Charlemagne et Arthur, ou le Roi imaginaire*
    (Paris, 1992)
Bryant, Nigel, *The Legend of the Grail* (Woodbridge, 2004)
Cardini, Franco, *Il Santo Graal* (Florence, 1997)
Castelnuovo, Enrico, ed., *Le stanze di Artu: Gli affreschi di frugarolo e
    l'immaginario cavalleresco nell'autumno del Medioevo* (Milan, 1999)
Chauou, A., *L'Idéologie Plantagenêt: Royauté arthurienne et monarchie
    politique dans l'espace Plantagenêt (XIIe–XIIIe siècles)* (Rennes, 2001)
Faral, Edmond, *La Légende arthurienne*, 3 vols (Paris, 1929)

Gardner, E. G., *The Arthurian Legend in Italian Literature* (London, 1930)

Geoffroy de Monmouth, *Histoire des rois de Bretagne*, trans. and ed. Laurence Mathey-Maille (Paris, 1992)

Loomis, R. S., *Arthurian Literature in the Middle Ages* (Oxford, 1959)

——, and L. H. Loomis, *Arthurian Legends in Medieval Art* (New York, 1938)

Marino, John B., *The Grail Legend in Modern Literature* (Woodbridge, 2004)

Markale, Jean, *Le Roi Arthur et la société celtique* (Paris, 1976)

Störmer, W., 'König Artus als aristokratisches Leitbild während des späten Mittelalters', *Zeitschrift für bayerische Landesgeschichte*, 35 (1972), pp. 946–71

Suard, François, 'Arthur', in *Dictionnaire encyclopédique du Moyen Âge*, ed. A. Vauchez (Paris, 1997), I, pp. 128–30

Whitaker, M., *The Legend of King Arthur in Art* (Cambridge, 1990)

THE CASTLE

Alcoy, Rose, 'Château', in *Dictionnaire critique d'iconographie occidentale*, ed. X. Barral i Altet (Rennes, 2003), pp. 185–8

Bonnassie, Pierre, 'Château', in *50 Mots clefs de l'histoire médiévale* (Toulouse, 1981), pp. 39–43

Boüard, Michel de, 'Les constructions militaires', *Manuel d'archéologie médiévale: De la fouille à l'histoire* (Paris, 1975), pp. 76–132

Brown, R. Allen, *English Castles* (London, 1962, rev. as *Allen Brown's English Castles*, 2004)

Bur, M., *Le Château*, Typologie des sources du Moyen Âge occidental 79 (Turnhout, 1999)

——, 'Château', in *Dictionnaire du Moyen Âge*, ed. Cl. Gauvard, A. de Libera and M. Zink (Paris, 2002), pp. 274–6

Caciagli, Giuseppe, *Il castello in Italia* (Florence, 1979)

Chapelot, Jean, *Le Château de Vincennes: Une résidence royale au Moyen Âge* (Paris, 1994)

Cuche, François-Xavier, *La Vie de château: Architecture, fonctions et représentations des châteaux et des palais du Moyen Âge à nos jours: Actes du colloque de Strasbourg* (Strasbourg, 1998)

Finó, José Federico, *Forteresses de la France médiévale* [1960], 3rd edn (Paris, 1977)

Bibliography

Fournier, Gabriel, *Le Château dans la France médiévale: Essai de sociologie monumentale* (Paris, 1978)

Gardelles, J., *Châteaux et guerriers de France au Moyen Âge*, IV: *Le Château expression du monde féodal* (Strasbourg, 1980)

Gieysztor, Aleksander, ed., *Zamek Królewski w Warszawie* [The Royal Castle of Warsaw] (Warsaw, 1973)

Hubert, J., and M.-Cl. Hubert, *Le Château fort* (Paris, 1965), nos 5–263

Laurent-Salch, Charles, ed., *L'Atlas des châteaux forts*, Centre d'études des châteaux forts de l'université de Strasbourg (Strasbourg, 1977); 4,969 castles still exist, of which 4,788 have been identified.

Licinio, R., *Castelli medievali: Puglia e basilica dai normanni a Federico II e Carlo I d'Angio* (Bari, 1994).

Merten, Klaus, ed., *Burgen und Schlösser in Deutschland* (Munich, 1995)

Mesqui, J., *Châteaux et enceintes de la France médiévale: De la défense à la résidence*, 2 vols (Paris, 1991–3)

Perdrizet, Marie-Pierre, *Le Moyen Âge au temps des chevaliers et des châteaux forts* (Paris, 1985)

Pesez, Jean-Marie, 'Château', in *Dictionnaire raisonné de l'Occident médiéval*, ed. J. Le Goff and J.-C. Schmitt (Paris, 1999), pp. 179–98

Poisson, Jean-Michel, ed., *Le Château médiéval, forteresse habitée (XIe–XVIe siècle)* (Paris, 1992)

Rapp, Francis, *Le Château fort dans la vie médiévale: Le château fort et la politique territoriale* (Strasbourg, 1968)

Rocolle, Pierre, *Le Temps des châteaux forts, Xe–XVe siècle* (Paris, 1994)

Tummers, Horst Johannes, *Rheinromantik: Romantik und Reisen am Rhein* (Cologne, 1968)

Wheatley, Abigail, *The Idea of the Castle in Medieval England* (York, 2004)

Willemsen, C. A., *Castel del Monte: Die Krone des Apuliens* (Wiesbaden, 1960)

THE CATHEDRAL

Les bâtisseurs de cathédrales, special issue of *L'Histoire* (December 2000)

La cathédrale, XIIe–XIVe siècle, Cahiers de Fanjeaux 30 (1995)

Les cathédrales de l'ouest de la France, special issue of *303. Arts, recherches et créations*, 70 (2001)

Toutes les cathédrales de France, special issue of *Notre histoire*
(July–August 1996)

20 siècles en cathédrales, exh. cat., ed, Catherine Arminjon and Denis Lavalle,
intro. Jacques Le Goff, Reims, Palais du Tau (2001)

Lumière gothique, I: *Cathédrales de France*; II: *Cathédrales d'Europe*,
Kairos Vision, CD-ROM, 1996

Clark, Kenneth, *The Gothic Revival: A Study in the History of Taste* (London,
1928)

Duby, Georges, *Le temps des cathédrales: L'art et la société, 980–1420*
(Paris, 1976), repr. in Duby, *L'Art et la Société : Moyen Âge–XXe siècle*
(Paris, 2002), pp. 453–1011

Du Colombier, Pierre, *Les chantiers des cathédrales* (Paris, 1973)

Erlande-Brandenburg, Alain, 'Cathédrale', in *Dictionnaire raisonné de
l'Occident médiéval*, ed. J.Le Goff and J.-C. Schmitt (Paris, 1999),
pp. 136–48

——, *La Cathédrale* (Paris, 1989)

——, *Notre-Dame de Paris* (Paris, 1991)

——, *Quand les cathédrales étaient peintes* (Paris, 1993)

Guénet, François, and Aline Kiner, *La Cathédrale livre de pierre*
(Paris, 2004)

Gy, Pierre-Marie, 'Ecclésiologie de la cathédrale', in *IX Centenário
de Dedicaçao da Sé de Braga: Braga, 18–22 October 1989*, III,
pp. 63–71

Kraus, Henry, *Gold was the Mortar: The Economics of Cathedral Building*
(London, 1979)

Recht, Roland, *Le croire et le voir: L'art des cathédrales (XIIe–XVe siècles)*
(Paris, 1999)

Sauerländer, Willibald, 'La cathédrale et la révolution', in *L'Art et les
révolutions: Acts du 27e Congrès international d'histoire de l'art,
Strasbourg, 1990*, pp. 67–106

Vauchez, André, 'La cathédrale', in *Les Lieux de mémoire*, III:
Les France, ed. Pierre Nora (Paris, 1992), pp. 91–127

CHARLEMAGNE

Charlemagne et l'épopée romane: Actes du VIIe congrès international de la Société Rencesvals, 1976 (Paris, 1978)

Charlemagne, père de l'Europe?, special issue of *Histoire médiévale*, 53 (May 2004)

Dalla storia al mito: la leggenda di Carlo Magno, special issue of *Medioevo*, 11 (November 2002)

La Saga de Charlemagne, trans. David W. Lacroix (Paris, 2000)

Barbero, Alessandro, *Charlemagne, Father of a Continent* [2000] (Berkeley, CA, Los Angeles and London, 2004)

Bathias-Rascalou, Céline, *Charlemagne et l'Europe* (Paris, 2004)

Bianchi, Giovanni, ed., *Eginardo, Vita di Carlo Magno*, intro. Claudio Leonardi (Rome 1980)

Boutet, Dominique, *Charlemagne et Arthur, ou le Roi imaginaire* (Paris, 1992)

Braunfels, Wolfgang, *Karl der Grosse: Lebenswerk und Nachleben*, 5 vols (Düsseldorf, 1965–8)

——, ed., *Karl der Grosse: Werk und Wirkung*, exh. cat. Aachen, Rathaus, 1965.

Eginhard [Einhard], *Early Lives of Charlemagne*, trans. A. J. Grant (London, 1900), available at www.yorku.ca/inpar/eginhard_grant.pdf, accessed 7 August 2019

Falkenstein, L., 'Charlemagne et Aix-la-Chapelle', *Byzantion*, 61 (1991), pp. 231–89

Favier, Jean, *Charlemagne* (Paris, 1999)

Folz, Robert, *Le Couronnement impérial de Charlemagne* (Paris, 1964)

——, *Le Souvenir et la Légende de Charlemagne dans l'Empire germanique médiéval* (Paris, 1950)

Graboïs, Arieh, 'Un mythe fondamental de l'histoire de France au Moyen Âge: le "roi David", précurseur du "roi très chrétien"', *Revue historique*, 287 (1992), pp. 11–31

Morrissey, Robert, *L'Empereur à la barbe fleurie: Charlemagne dans la mythologie et l'histoire de France* (Paris, 1997); Eng. trans. as *Charlemagne and France: A Thousand Years of Mythology* (Notre Dame, IN, 2003)

Paris, Gaston, *Histoire poétique de Charlemagne* [1865] (Paris, 1905, repr. Geneva, 1974)

Rader, Olaf B., *Grab und Herrschaft: Politischer Totenkult von Alexander dem Grossen bis Lenin* (Munich, 2003)

Ratkowitsch, Christine, *Karolus Magnus: alter Ænea, alter Martinus, alter Iustinus. Zu Intention und Datierung des 'Aachener Karlsepos'* (Vienna, 1997)

EL CID

Cantar de mío Cid. Chanson de mon Cid, trans. Jules Horrent, 2 vols (Ghent, 1982)

Chanson de mon Cid. Cantar de mío Cid, ed. and trans. Georges Martin (Paris, 1996)

The Song of the Cid, ed. María Rosa Menocal, trans. Burton Raffel (London, 2009)

Aurell, Martin, 'Cid (Le)', in *Dictionnaire encyclopédique du Moyen Âge*, ed. A. Vauchez (Paris, 1997), I, p. 329

Epalza, M. de, and S. Guellouz, *Le Cid, personnage historique et littéraire* (Paris, 1983)

Fletcher, Richard, *The Quest for El Cid* (Oxford, 1989)

Lacarra, María Eugenia, *El Poema de mío Cid: realidad histórica e ideología* (Madrid, 1980)

Menéndez Pidal, Ramón, *La España del Cid* (Madrid, 1929)

Menjot, Denis, 'Cid (Le)', in *Dictionnaire du Moyen Âge*, ed. Cl. Gauvard, A. de Libera and M. Zink (Paris, 2002), p. 291

Smith, Colin, *The Making of the 'Poema de mío Cid'* (Cambridge, 1983)

THE CLOISTER

Braunfels, Wolfgang, *Abendländische Klosterbaukunst* (Cologne, 1969)

Carron-Touchard, Jacqueline, *Cloîtres romans de France* (La Pierre-qui-Vire, 1983)

Evans, Joan, *Monastic Life at Cluny, 910–1157* (Oxford, 1931)

Gerhards, Agnès, 'Clôture', in *Dictionnaire historique des ordres religieux* (Paris, 1998), pp. 160–62

Goetz, Hans-Werner, 'Kloster und Mönschleben', *Leben im Mittelalter vom 7 bis zum 13. Jahrhundert* (Munich, 1986), pp. 65–113

Jacobsen, Werner, *Der Klosterplan von St. Gallen und die karolingische Architektur* (Berlin, 1992)

Klein, Peter K., ed., *Der mittelalterliche Kreuzgang. The Medieval Cloisters. Le Cloître du Moyen Âge: Architektur, Funktion und Programm* (Regensburg, 2004)

Leclercq, Henri, 'Cloître', in *Dictionnaire d'archéologie chrétienne et de liturgie* (Paris, 1914), III/2, pp. 1991–2012

Lopez, Élisabeth, 'Clôture', in *Dictionnaire encyclopédique du Moyen Âge*, ed. A. Vauchez (Paris, 1997), I, pp. 346–7

Mallet, Géraldine, 'Cloître', in *Dictionnaire critique d'iconographie occidentale*, ed. X. Barral i Altet (Rennes, 2003), pp. 210–12

Miccoli, Giovanni, 'Les moines', in *L'Homme médiéval*, ed. J. Le Goff (Paris, 1989), pp. 45–85

Moulin, Léo, *La vie quotidienne des religieux au Moyen Âge, Xe–XVe s.* (Paris, 1978)

Pressouyre, Léon, 'St Bernard to St Francis: Monastic Ideals and Iconographic Programs in the Cloister', *Gesta*, XII (1973), pp. 71–92

THE JONGLEUR

Le Moyen Âge, entre ordre et désordre, exh. cat., Paris, Cité de la musique à la Villette, 2004, esp. Martine Clouzot, pp. 56–7

Baldwin, John W., 'The Image of the Jongleur in Northern France around 1200', *Speculum*, LXXII/3 (1997), pp. 635–63

Casagrande, Carla, and Silvana Vecchio, 'Clercs et jongleurs dans la société médiévale (XIIe–XIIIe siècle)', *Annales ESC*, XXXIV/5 (1979), pp. 913–28

Charles-Dominique, Luc, 'Du jongleur au ménétrier: Évolution du statut central des instrumentistes médiévaux', in *Instruments à cordes du Moyen Âge*, ed. Ch. Rault (Grâne, 1999), pp. 29–47

Clouzot, Martine, '*Homo ludens, homo viator*: le jongleur au cœur des échanges culturels au Moyen Âge', *Actes du XXXIIe congrès de la SHMESP: Boulogne-sur-Mer, 2001*, pp. 293–301

——, and Isabelle Marchesin, *Le jongleur au Moyen Âge* (Paris, 2001)

Faral, E., *Les jongleurs en France au Moyen Âge* (Paris, 1910)

Hartung, W., *Die Spielleute: Eine Randgruppe in der Gesellschaft des Mittelalters* (Wiesbaden, 1982)

Marchesin, Isabelle, 'Les jongleurs dans les psautiers du haut Moyen Âge: nouvelles hypothèses sur la symbolique de l'histoire médiévale', *Cahiers de civilisation médiévale*, 41 (1998), pp. 127–39

Rychner, J., *La chanson de geste: Essai sur l'art épique des jongleurs* (Geneva, 1967)

Stanesco, Michel, 'Jongleur', in *Dictionnaire encyclopédique du Moyen Âge*, ed. A. Vauchez (Paris, 1997), I, p. 83

Zink, Michel, *Le Jongleur de Notre-Dame: Contes chrétiens du Moyen Âge* (Paris, 1999)

—, *Littérature française du Moyen Âge* (Paris, 1992)

—, *Poésie et conversion au Moyen Âge* (Paris, 2003), pp. 161–3, 173–4

Zumthor, Paul, *La lettre et la voix: De la 'littérature' médiévale* (Paris, 1987)

KNIGHTS AND CHIVALRY

Arnold, B., *German Knighthood, 1050–1300* (Oxford, 1985)

Barber, Richard, and Juliet Barker, *Tournaments: Jousts, Chivalry and Pageants in the Middle Ages* [1989] (Woodbridge, rev. 2013)

Barthélemy, Dominique, 'Modern Mythologies of Medieval Chivalry', in *Medieval World*, ed. P. Linehan and J. Nelson (London, 2001), pp. 214–28

Borst, Arno, ed., *Das Rittertum im Mittelalter* (Darmstadt, 1976)

Bumke, Joachim, *Studien zum Ritterbegriff im 12. und 13. Jarhhundert* (Heidelberg, 1964)

Cardini, Franco, 'Le guerrier et le chevalier', in *L'Homme médiéval*, ed. J. Le Goff (Paris, 1984), pp. 87–128

Chênerie, Marie-Luce, *Le Chevalier errant dans les romans arthuriens en vers des XIIe et XIIIe siècles* (Geneva, 1986)

Curtius, Ernst Robert, 'The Chivalric System of the Virtues', in *European Literature and the Late Middle Ages* [1948] (Princeton, NJ, 1990), pp. 519–37

Demurger, Alain, *Chevaliers du Christ: Les ordres religieux militaires au Moyen Âge, XIe–XVIe siècle* (Paris, 2002)

De Smedt, Raphael, ed., *Les Chevaliers de l'ordre de la Toison d'or au XVe siècle: Notices bio-bibliographiques*, 2nd edn (Frankfurt, 2000)

Duby, Georges, *Guillaume le Maréchal, le meilleur chevalier du monde* (Paris, 1984); repr. in Duby, *Féodalité* (Paris, 1996), pp. 1051–160; as *William Marshal: The Flower of Chivalry*, trans. Richard Howard (New York, 1985)

——, *La société chevaleresque* (Paris, 1988); repr. in Duby, *Qu'est-ce que la société féodale?* (Paris, 2002), pp. 1051–205

——, *Le dimanche de Bouvines* (Paris, 1973); as *The Legend of Bouvines: War, Religion, and Culture in the Middle Ages*, trans. Catherine Tihanyi (Berkeley, CA, 1990)

Fleckenstein, Josef, ed., *Das ritterliche Turnier in Mittelalter* (Göttingen, 1985)

Flori, Jean, *Brève histoire de la chevalerie: De l'histoire au mythe chevaleresque* (Monsempron Libos, 1999)

——, 'Chevalerie', in *Dictionnaire raisonné de l'Occident médiéval*, ed. J. Le Goff and J.-Cl. Schmitt (Paris, 1999), pp. 199–213

——, *La Chevalerie* (Paris, 1998)

——, *L'Idéologie du glaive: Préhistoire de la chevalerie* (Geneva, 1983)

——, *Richard the Lionheart: King and Knight* [1999] (Edinburgh, 2006)

Frappier, Jean, *Amour courtois et Table Ronde* (Geneva, 1973)

Girouard, Mark, *The Return to Camelot: Chivalry and the English Gentleman* (New Haven, CT, and London, 1981)

Keen, M., *Chivalry* (New Haven, CT, 1984)

Köhler, Erich, *Ideal und Wirklichkeit in der höfischen Epik* (Tübingen, 1970, repr. 2011)

Le Rider, Paule, *Le Chevalier dans le 'Conte du Graal' de Chrétien de Troyes* (Paris, 1978)

Marchello-Nizia, Christiane, 'Amour courtois, société masculine et figures du pouvoir', in *Annales ESC* (1981), pp. 969–82

Painter, Sidney, *French Chivalry* (Ithaca, NY, 1957)

Paravicini, Werner, *Die ritterlich-höfische Kultur des Mittelalters* (Munich, 1994)

Perdrizet, Marie-Pierre, *Le Moyen Âge au temps des chevaliers et des châteaux forts* (Paris, 1985)

Rabeyroux, Anne, 'Chevalier', in *Dictionnaire critique d'iconographie occidentale*, ed. X. Barral i Altet (Rennes, 2003), pp. 192–3

——, *Richard Cœur de Lion: Histoire et légende* (Paris, 1989)

Roubaud-Bénichou, Sylvia, *Le Roman de chevalerie en Espagne: Entre Arthur et Don Quichotte* (Paris, 2000)

Ruiz-Doménec, José Enrique, *La caballería, o, La imagen cortesana del mundo* (Genoa, 1984)

Stanesco, Michel, *Jeux d'errance du chevalier médiéval, aspects ludiques de la fonction guerrière dans la littérature du Moyen Âge flamboyant* (Leiden, 1988)

Vale, M., *War and Chivalry* (London, 1981)

Vernier, Richard, *The Flower of Chivalry: Bertrand du Guesclin and the Hundred Years War* (Woodbridge, 2003)

THE LAND OF COCKAIGNE

Texts

Boccaccio, Giovanni, *Decameron*, VIII.3

Camposesi, P., 'Il piacevole viaggio di Cuccagna', appendix to 'Carnevale, Cuccagna e giuochi di villa', *Studi e problemi di critica testuale*, 10 (1975), pp. 57–97 (93–7); repr. in *Il paese della fame*, 2nd edn (Bologne, 1985), pp. 212–16

Dunn, Charles W., and Edward T. Byrnes, 'The Land of Cokaygne', *Middle English Literature* (New York, 1973), pp. 188–92

Haupt, Moriz, and Heinrich Hoffmann, eds, 'Vom Schlaraffenland', *Altdeutsche Blätter* (Leipzig, 1836), I, pp. 163–70

Pleit, Herman, *Dreaming of Cockaigne: Medieval Fantasies of the Perfect Life* [1987] (New York, 2001)

Sachs, Hans, 'Das Schlaraffenland', in *Sämtliche Fabeln und Schwänke*, ed. Edmund Goetze and Carl Drescher (Halle, 1893), I, pp. 8–11

Väänänen, Veikko, ed., 'Le "Fabliau" de Cocagne', *Neuphilologische Mitteilungen*, XLVIII/1 (1947), pp. 3–36

Studies

Ackermann, Elfriede, *Das Schlaraffenland in German Literature and Folksong: Social Aspects of an Earthly Paradise* (Chicago, IL, 1944)

Borgnet, G., 'Le pays de Cocagne dans la littérature allemande, des origines à Hans Sachs', in Danielle Buschinger, Wolfgang Spiewok, ed., *Gesellschaftsutopien im Mittelalter/Discours et figures de l'utopie*

au Moyen Âge: Actes du ve Congrès annuel de la Société Reineke
   (Greifswald, 1994), pp. 15–27

Cocchiara, Giuseppe, *Il mondo alla rovescia* (Turin, 1963)

——, *Il paese di Cuccagna e altri studi di folklore* [1956] (Turin, 1980)

Delpech, F., 'Aspects des pays de Cocagne, programmes pour une
   recherche', in *L'Image du monde renversé et ses représentations littéraires
   et paralittéraires de la fin du XVIe s. au milieu du XVIIe*, ed. Jean Lafond
   and Augustin Redeno (Paris, 1979), pp. 35–48

Delumeau, J., *La mort des pays de Cocagne* (Paris, 1976)

Franco Júnior, Hilário, *Cocanha: A Historia de une pais imaginário*
   (São Paulo, 1998); Fr. trans. as *Cocagne: Histoire d'un pays imaginaire*,
   preface by Jacques Le Goff (Paris, 2013)

Le Goff, Jacques, 'L'utopie médiévale: le pays de Cocagne', *Revue européenne
   des sciences sociales*, XXVII/85 (1989), pp. 271–86

Graf, A., 'Il paese du Cuccagna e i paradisi artificiali', in *Miti, leggende et
   superstizioni del Medioevo* (Milan, 1892–3)

Graus, F., 'Social Utopias in the Middle Ages', *Past and Present*, 38 (1967),
   pp. 3–19

Trousson, R., *Voyages aux pays de nulle part: Histoire littéraire de la pensée
   utopique* (Brussels, 1975)

MELUSINA

Boivin, J.-M., and P. MacCana, ed., *Mélusines continentales et insulaires*
   (Paris, 1999)

Clier-Colombani, Françoise, *La Fée Mélusine au Moyen Âge. Images, mythes
   et symboles* (Paris, 1881)

Coudrette, *Le Roman de Mélusine*, trans. Laurence Harf-Lancner
   (Paris, 1993)

Harf-Lancner, Laurence, 'La vraie histoire de la fée Mélusine', *L'Histoire*, 119
   (1989), pp. 8–15

——, *Le monde des fées dans l'Occident médiéval* (Paris, 2003)

——, 'Le mythe de Mélusine', in *Dictionnaire des mythes littéraires*,
   ed. P. Brunel (Paris, 1988), pp. 999–1004

——, *Les fées au Moyen Âge: Morgane et Mélusine; la naissance des fées*,
   2nd edn (Paris, 1991)

Jean d'Arras, *Mélusine (le Roman de Mélusine ou l'histoire des Lusignan)*,
    trans. Michèle Perret, preface by Jacques Le Goff (Paris, 1979)
—, *Mélusine ou la Noble Histoire de Lusignan*, ed. and trans. Jean-Jacques
    Vincensini (Paris, 2003)
Lecouteux, Claude, 'La structure des légendes mélusiniennes', in
    Annales ESC, XXXIII/2 (1978), pp. 294–306
—, *Mélusine et le Chevalier au Cygne*, preface by Jacques Le Goff
    (Paris, 1982)
Le Goff, Jacques, with E. Le Roy Ladurie, 'Mélusine maternelle et
    défricheuse', *Annales ESC*, XXVI/3 (1971), pp. 587–622; repr. in
    Pour un autre Moyen Âge (Paris, 1977), pp. 307–31
Lund, Bea, *Melusine und Merlin im Mittelalter: Entwürfe und Modelle
    weiblicher Existenz im Beziehungsdiskurs der Geschlechter* (Munich,
    1991)
Maddox, Donald, and Sara Sturm-Maddox, *Melusine of Lusignan: Founding
    Fiction in Late Medieval France* (Athens, GA, 1996)
*Mélusine: Actes du colloque du Centre d'études médiévales de l'université de
    Picardie Jules Verne, January, 1996.*
Pillard, Guy-Édouard, *La Déesse Mélusine: Mythologie d'une fée*
    (Maulévrier, 1989)
Pinto-Mathieu, Élisabeth, *Le Roman de Mélusine de Coudrette et son
    adaptation allemande dans le roman en prose de Thüring von
    Ringoltingen* (Göppingen, 1990)
Sergent, Bernard, 'Cinq études sur Mélusine', *Mythologie française*, 177
    (1995), pp. 27–38
Thüring de Ringoltingen, *Mélusine et autres récits*, trans. and ed. Claude
    Lecouteux (Paris, 1999)
Vincensini, Jean-Jacques, 'Mélusine ou la vertu de la trahison (notes sur la
    vraisemblance dans les récits mélusiniens)', *Revue des langues romanes*,
    CII/2 (1996), pp. 35–48
—, 'Modernité de Mélusine dans *Le Dernier Chant de Malaterre*
    de François Bourgeon', in *La France médiévale et les écrivains
    d'aujourd'hui*, ed. M. Gally (Paris, 2000), pp. 163–78

MERLIN

Baumgartner, Emmanuelle, *Merlin le prophète ou Livre du Graal* (Paris, 1980)

Berthelot, Anne, 'Merlin', in *Dictionnaire du Moyen Âge*, ed. Cl. Gauvard, A. de Libera and M. Zink (Paris, 2002), pp. 903–4

Bloch, R. H., 'Merlin and the Modes of Medieval Legal Meaning', in *Archéologie des signes*, ed. Lucie Brind'Amour and Eugène Vance (Toronto, 1983), pp. 127–44

Harding, C. A., *Merlin and Legendary Romance* (New York and London, 1988)

Micha, Alexandre, 'Merlin', in *Dictionnaire des lettres françaises: Le Moyen Âge* (Paris, 1964), pp. 1098–9

——, ed., *Merlin* (Geneva, 1980)

Reeves, Marjorie, *The Influence of Prophecy in the Later Middle Ages: A Study in Joachimism* (Oxford, 1969)

Rusconi, Roberto, *Profezia e profeti alla fine del Medioevo* (Rome, 1999)

Suard, François, 'Merlin', in *Dictionnaire encyclopédique du Moyen Âge*, ed. A. Vauchez (Paris, 1997), II, p. 989

Vauchez, André, ed., *Les textes prophétiques et la prophétie en Occident (xiie–xvie siècles)* (Rome, 1990)

Zumthor, Paul, *Merlin le prophète: un thème de la littérature prophétique de l'historiographie et des romans* (Lausanne, 1943, repr. Geneva, 2000)

POPE JOAN

Boureau, Alain, *La Papesse Jeanne* (Paris, 1988)

Döllinger, Ignaz von, *Die Papst-Fabeln des Mittelalters: Ein Beitrag zur Kirchengeschichte* (Munich, 1863, rev. Stuttgart, 1890); trans. Alfred Plummer as *Dr. J.J.I. Döllinger's Fables Respecting the Popes in the Middle Ages* (New York, 1872)

Onofrio, Cesare d', *La papessa Giovanna: Roma e papato tra storia et leggende* (Rome, 1979)

Paravicini Bagliani, Agostino, *The Pope's Body*, trans. David S. Peterson [1994] (Chicago, IL, 1999)

Pardoe, Rosemary, and Darroll Pardoe, *The Female Pope: The Mystery of Pope Joan* (Wellingborough, 1988)

Petoia, Erberto, 'Scandalo a San Pietro', *Medioevo*, 87 (April 2004), pp. 69–73

REYNARD

Texts

Fuchs Reinhart, Fr. trans. Danielle Buschinger and Jean-Marc Pastré (Greifswald, 1993)

Le Goupil et le Paysan (Roman de Renart, branche x), ed. Jean Dufournet (Paris, 1990)

Le Roman de Renart, ed. and trans. Jean Dufournet and André Méline, 2 vols (Paris, 1985)

Le Roman de Renart, ed. and trans. Armand Strubel (Paris, 1998)

Le Roman d'Ysengrin, trans. E. Charbonnier (Paris, 1991)

L'Évasion d'un prisonnier/ Ecbasis cujusdam captivi, ed. and trans. C. Munier (Paris, 1998)

Reinhart Fuchs, trans. W. Spiewok (Leipzig, 1977)

Une œuvre: Le Roman de Renart: un thème: société animale et société humaine, ed. Annik Arnaldi and Noëlle Anglade (Paris, 1977)

Studies

Reinardus: Yearbook of the International Reynard Society (1988–)

'Renart', *Lexicon des Mittelalters* (Munich, 1977–98), VII, col. 720–24

Batany, Jean, *Scènes et Coulisses du Roman de Renart* (Paris, 1989)

Bellon, Roger, 'Roman de Renart', in *Dictionnaire du Moyen Âge*, ed. Cl. Gauvard, A. de Libera and M. Zink (Paris, 2002), pp. 1243–4

——, 'Trickery as an Element of Character of Renart', *Forum for Modern Language Studies*, XXII/1 (1986), pp. 34–52

Bossuat, Robert, *Le Roman de Renard*, 2nd edn (Paris, 1967)

——, and Sylvie Lefèvre, 'Roman de Renart', in *Dictionnaire des lettres françaises: Le Moyen Âge* [1964] (Paris, 1992), pp. 1312–15

Combarieu du Grès, Micheline, and Jean Dubrénat, *Le Roman de Renart: index des thèmes et des personnages* (Aix-en-Provence, 1987)

Delort, Robert, *Les animaux ont une histoire* (Paris, 1984)

Dragonetti, Roger, 'Renart est mort, Renart est vif, Renart règne', *Critique*, 34 (1978), pp. 783–98; repr. in *La Musique et les Lettres* (Geneva, 1986), pp. 419–34

Flinn, J., *Le Roman de Renart dans la littérature française et dans les littératures étrangères au Moyen Âge* (Paris and Toronto, 1963)

Foulet, Lucien, *Le Roman de Renard* (Paris, 1914)

Goullet, Monique, 'Ecbasis cujusdam captivi', in *Dictionnaire du Moyen Âge*, ed. Cl. Gauvard, A. de Libera and M. Zink (Paris, 2002), p. 458

Pastré, Jean-Marc, '*Reinhart Fuchs*', in *Dictionnaire du Moyen Âge*, ed. Cl. Gauvard, A. de Libera and M. Zink (Paris, 2002), pp. 1192–4

Reichler, Claude, *La Diabolie: la séduction, la renardie, l'écriture* (Paris, 1979)

Rivals, Claude, ed., *Le Rire de Goupil: Renard, prince de l'entre-deux* (Toulouse, 1998)

Roussel, Henri, '*Renart le Nouvel*' de Jacquemart Gielie: Étude littéraire (Lille, 1984)

Scheidegger, J., *Le Roman de Renart ou le Texte de la dérision* (Geneva, 1989)

Strubel, Armand, *La Rose, Renart et le Graal* (Paris, 1989)

Tilliette, Jean-Yves, 'Ysengrinus', in *Dictionnaire du Moyen Âge*, ed. Cl. Gauvard, A. de Libera and M. Zink (Paris, 2002), p. 1483

Varty, Kenneth, *Reynard the Fox: A Study of the Fox in Medieval English Art* (Leicester, 1967)

Voisenet, Jacques, *Bestiaire chrétien: L'imagerie animale des auteurs du haut-Moyen Âge (Ve–XIe siècle)* (Toulouse, 1994)

——, *Bêtes et hommes dans le monde médiéval: Le bestiaire des clercs du Ve au XIIe siècle*, preface by Jacques Le Goff (Turnhout, 2000)

ROBIN HOOD

Dobson, R. B., and J. Taylor, *Rymes of Robin Hood: An Introduction to the English Outlaw* (London, 1976)

Gleissner, R., 'Robin Hood', in *Lexicon des Mittelalters* (Munich, 1977–98), VII, cols 919–20

Holt, J. C., *Robin Hood* (London, 1982)

Pollard, A. J., *Imagining Robin Hood: The Late Medieval Stories in Historical Context* (Woodbridge, 2004)

ROLAND

Texts

La chanson de Roland, ed. and trans. Joseph Bédier, 6th edn (Paris, 1938)

La chanson de Roland, ed. and trans. Gérard Moignet, 3rd edn (Paris, 1972)

La chanson de Roland, ed. and trans. Pierre Jonin (Paris, 1979)

La chanson de Roland, ed. and trans. Jan Short (Paris, 1990)

La chanson de Roland, ed. and trans. Jean Dufournet (Paris, 1993)

La chanson de Roland, ed. Cesare Segre [1971] (Geneva, 2003)

La Chanson de Roland / The Song of Roland: The French Corpus, ed. Joseph J. Duggan (Turnhout, 2005)

Studies

Amalvi, Christian, 'La *Chanson de Roland* et l'image de Roland dans la littérature scolaire en France de 1815 à 1914', in *De l'art et la manière d'accommoder les héros de l'histoire de France: De Vercingétorix à la Révolution* (Paris, 1988), pp. 89–111

Burger, A., *Turold, poète de la fidélité* (Geneva, 1977)

Dufournet, Jean, *Cours sur la Chanson de Roland* (Paris, 1972)

Galletti, Anna Imelda, and Roberto Roda, *Sulle orme di Orlando: Leggende e luoghi carolingi in Italia: I paladini di Francia nella tradizioni italiane: Una proposta storico-anthropologica* (Padua, 1987)

Horrent, Jules, 'Roland (Chanson de)', in *Dictionnaire des lettres françaises: Le Moyen Âge* (Paris, 1992), pp. 1299–1304

Keller, H.-E., *Autour de Roland: Recherches sur la chanson de geste* (Paris, 1989)

Lafont, Robert, *La Geste de Roland*, 2 vols (Paris, 1991)

Le Gentil, Pierre, *La Chanson de Roland* (Paris, 1955)

Lejeune, Rita, 'Le héros Roland, mythe ou personnage historique?', *Académie royale de Belgique: Bulletin de la classe des lettres et des sciences morales et politiques*, 5th ser., LXV (1979), pp. 145–65

——, and Jacques Stiennon, 'Le héros Roland, "neveu de Charlemagne", dans iconographie médiévale', in *Karl der Grosse: Lebenswerk und Nachleben*, ed. Wolfgang Braunfels (Düsseldorf, 1965–8), IV, pp. 215–28

——, and Jacques Stiennon, *The Legend of Roland in the Middle Ages*, 2 vols [1966] (London, 1971)

Mandach, A. de, *La Chanson de Roland, transfert du mythe dans le monde occidental et oriental* (Geneva, 1993)

Menéndez Pidal, Ramón, *La Chanson de Roland et la tradition épique des Francs* (Paris, 1960)

Roncaglia, Aurelio, 'Roland e il peccato di Carlomagno' [1986], in *Epica francese medievale* (Rome, 2012), pp. 75–104

Roques, Mario, 'L'attitude du héros mourant dans *La Chanson de Roland*', *Romania*, LXVI (1940), pp. 355–66

TRISTAN AND ISEULT

Texts

Bédier, Joseph, *Le Roman de Tristan et Iseut* (Paris, 1900)

Béroul, *Tristan et Yseut*, ed. Daniel Poirion, preface by Christiane Marchello-Nizia (Paris, 1995)

Mary, André, *La Merveilleuse Histoire de Tristan et Iseut*, preface by Denis de Rougemont (Paris, 1973)

Tristan et Iseut: Les 'Tristan' en vers, ed. and trans. Jean-Charles Payen (Paris, 1974)

Tristan et Iseut: Les poèmes français, la saga norroise, trans. Philippe Walter and Daniel Lacroix (Paris, 1989)

Tristan et Yseut: Les premières versions européennes, ed. Christiane Marchello-Nizia (Paris, 1995)

Studies

Baumgartner, Emmanuelle, *La Harpe et l'Épée: Tradition et renouvellement dans le 'Tristan' en prose* (Paris, 1990)

—, *Tristan et Iseut: De la légende aux récits en vers* (Paris, 1987)

Buschinger, Danielle, ed., *La Légende de Tristan au Moyen Âge* (Göttingen, 1982)

Cazenave, Michel, *Le Philtre et l'Amour: La légende de Tristan et Iseut* (Paris, 1969)

—, ed., *Tristan et Yseut, mythe européen et mondial* (Göttingen, 1987)

Chocheyras, Jacques, *Tristant et Iseut: Genèse d'un mythe littéraire* (Paris, 1996)

Frappier, Jean, 'Structure et sens du Tristan: version commune, version courtoise', *Cahiers de civilisation médiévale*, 6 (1963), pp. 255–80, 441–54

Fritz, Jean-Marie, 'Tristan (légende de)' and 'Tristan en prose', in
    Dictionnaire des lettres françaises. Le Moyen Âge, 2nd edn (Paris, 1991),
    pp. 1445–8, 1448–50
Heijkant, Marie-José, ed., *Tristano Riccardiano* (Parma, 1991)
Kleinhenz, C., 'Tristan in Italy: The Death or Rebirth of a Legend', *Studies
    in Medieval Culture*, 5 (1975), pp. 145–58
Lejeune, Rita, 'Les noms de Tristan et Iseut dans l'anthroponymie médiévale',
    in *Mélanges offerts à Jean Frappier* (Geneva, 1970), II, pp. 525–630
Miquel, André, *Deux histoires d'amour, de Majnūn à Tristan* (Paris, 1995)
Pastoureau, Michel, 'Les armoiries de Tristan', in *L'Hermine et le Sinople:
    Études d'héraldisme médiéval* (Paris, 1982), pp. 279–98
Payen, Jean-Charles, 'Lancelot contre Tristan: La conjuration d'un mythe
    subversif (Réflexions sur l'idéologie romanesque au Moyen Âge)',
    in *Mélanges de langue et de littérature médiévales offerts à Pierre Le
    Gentil* (Paris, 1973), pp. 617–32
Poirion, Daniel, 'Le Tristan de Béroul: récit, légende et mythe',
    L'Information littéraire, XXVI (1974), pp. 159–207
Ribard, Jacques, *Du philtre au Graal: Pour une interprétation théologique
    du roman de 'Tristan' et du 'Conte du Graal'* (Geneva, 1989)
Rougemont, Denis de, *L'Amour et l'Occident* (Paris, 1972)
Wagner, Richard, *Tristan et Isolde*, trans. Pierre Miquel, preface by Pierre
    Boulez (Paris, 1996)
Walter, Philippe, *Le Gant de verre: Le mythe de Tristan et Yseut*
    (La Gacilly, 1990)

TROUBADOURS AND TROUVÈRES

Music

Aubrey, Elizabeth, *The Music of the Troubadours* (Bloomington, IN, 1996)
Werf, Hendrik van der, *The Extant Troubadour Melodies: Transcriptions
    and Essays for Performers and Scholars*, ed. Gerald A. Bond
    (Rochester, NY, 1984)

Texts

Aurell, Martin, *La Vielle et l'Épée: Troubadours et politique en Provence au
    XIIIe siècle* (Paris, 1989)

Bec, Pierre, *Anthologie des troubadours*, 2nd edn (Paris, 1985)

——, *Burlesque et obscénité chez les troubadours* (Paris, 1984)

Boutière, Jean, et al., *Biographies des troubadours: Textes provençaux des XIIIe et XIVe siècles*, 2nd edn (Paris, 1973)

Jeanroy, A., *Anthologie des troubadours, XIIe et XIIIe siècles* (Paris, 1974)

Lavaud, R., and R. Nelli, *Les Troubadours*, 2 vols (Bruges, 1960–66)

Riquer, Martin de, *Los Trovadores: historia literaria y textos*, 3 vols (Barcelona, 1975)

Rosenberg, S. N., H. Tischler and G. Grossel, *Chansons de trouvères: 'Chanter m'estuet'* (Paris, 1995)

Studies

Brunel-Lobrichon, Geneviève, 'Troubadours', in *Dictionnaire des lettres françaises. Le Moyen Âge* (Paris, 1992), pp. 1456–8

——, and Claudie Duhamel-Amado, *Au temps des troubadours, XIIe–XIIIe siècle* (Paris, 1997)

Cheyette, Fredric L., *Ermengard of Narbonne and the World of the Troubadours* (Ithaca, NY, 2001)

Cropp, Glynnis M., *Le vocabulaire courtois des troubadours de l'époque classique* (Geneva, 1975)

Huchet, Jean-Claude, *L'Amour discourtois: La 'fine amor' chez les premiers troubadours* (Toulouse, 1987)

——, 'Vidas et razos', in *Dictionnaire du Moyen Âge*, ed. Cl. Gauvard, A. de Libera and M. Zink (Paris, 2002), pp. 1446–7

Kay, Sarah, *Subjectivity in Troubadour Poetry* (Cambridge, 1990)

Köhler, Erich, 'Observations historiques et sociologiques sur la poésie des troubadours', *Cahiers de civilisation médiévale*, VI (1964), pp. 27–51

——, *Trobadorlyrik und höfischer Roman* (Berlin, 1962); Fr. trans. as *L'Aventure chevaleresque: Idéal et réalité dans le roman courtois*, preface by Jacques Le Goff (Paris, 1974)

Marrou, Henri-Irénée (Davenson), *Les Troubadours* (Paris, 1971)

Monson, Don A., 'The Troubadour's Lady Reconsidered Again', *Speculum*, LXX/2 (1995), pp. 255–74

Muraille, Guy, 'Trouvères lyriques', in *Dictionnaire des lettres françaises. Le Moyen Âge* (Paris, 1992), pp. 1458–63

Nelli, René, *Écrivains anti-conformistes du Moyen Âge occitan*, 2 vols (Paris, 1977)

—, *L'Érotique des troubadours*, 2 vols (Paris, 1974)

Paden, William D., 'The Troubadour's Lady as Seen through Thick History', *Exemplaria*, XI/2 (1999), pp. 221–44

—, ed., *The Voice of the Trobairitz: Perspectives on the Women Troubadours* (Philadelphia, PA, 1989)

Paterson, Linda, *The World of the Troubadours: Medieval Occitan Society, c. 1100–1300* (Cambridge, 1993)

Payen, Jean-Charles, *Le Prince d'Aquitaine : Essai sur Guillaume IX, son œuvre et son érotique* (Paris, 1980)

Régnier-Bohler, Danielle, 'Amour courtois', in *Dictionnaire raisonné de l'Occident médiéval*, ed. J. Le Goff and J.-Cl. Schmitt (Paris, 1999), pp. 32–41

Roubaud, Jacques, *La Fleur inverse: Essais sur l'art formel des troubadours* (Paris, 1986)

—, *Les Troubadours* (Paris, 1980)

Warning, Rainer, 'Moi lyrique et société chez les troubadours', in *Archéologie des signes*, ed. Lucie Brind'Amour and Eugène Vance (Toronto, 1983), pp. 63–100

Zuccheto, Gérard, *Terre des troubadours (XIIe–XIIIe siècle)*, preface by Max Rouquette (Paris, 1996, with CD)

THE UNICORN

Astorg, B. d', *Le mythe de la Dame à la Licorne* (Paris, 1963)

Bersier, J., *Jean Duvet, le Maître à la Licorne* (Paris, 1977)

Bianciotto, G., *Bestiaire du Moyen Âge* (Paris, 1980)

Boudet, J.-P., *La Dame à la Licorne* (Toulouse, 1999)

Carmody, F. J., 'Physiologus latinus version Y', *University of California Publications in Classical Philology*, XII/7 (1941), pp. 95–137

Chiellini Nari, Monica, 'Licorne', in *Dictionnaire encyclopédique du Moyen Âge*, ed. A. Vauchez (Paris, 1997), II, pp. 893–4

Erlande-Brandenburg, Alain, et C. Rose, *La Dame à la Licorne* (Paris, 1993)

Gay, Victor, and Henri Stern, 'Licorne', in *Glossaire archéologique du Moyen Âge et de la Renaissance*, 2 vols (Paris, 1885), II, pp. 76–8

Gotfredsen, Lise, *The Unicorn* (London, 1999)

Guglielmi, N., *El Fisiologo, bestiario medieval* (Buenos Aires, 1971)

Henkel, Nikolaus, *Studien zum Physiologus im Mittelalter* (Tübingen, 1976), esp. pp. 168–71

Jacquart, Danielle, 'Physiologus', in *Dictionnaire encyclopédique du Moyen Âge*, ed. A. Vauchez (Paris, 1997), II, pp. 1209–10

Joubert, Fabienne, *La tapisserie médiévale au Musée de Cluny*, 3rd edn (Paris, 2002)

Kendrick, A. L., 'Quelques remarques sur la "Dame à la Licorne" du Musée de Cluny (allégorie des cinq sens?)', *Actes du congrès d'Histoire de l'art, Paris, 1921*, III, pp. 662–6

Maurice, Jean, 'Bestiaires', in *Dictionnaire du Moyen Âge*, ed. Cl. Gauvard, A. de Libera and M. Zink (Paris, 2002), pp. 161–3

Planche, Alice, 'Deux monstres ambigus: licorne et lycanthrope', in *Démons et Merveilles au Moyen Âge: Colloque international de Nice, 1987*, pp. 153–70

Reynaud, Nicole, 'Un peintre français, cartonnier de tapisserie au XVe siècle, Henri de Valay', *Revue de l'art*, 22 (1973), pp. 6–21

Schneebalg-Perelman, S., 'La Dame à la licorne a été tissée à Bruxelles', *Gazette des beaux-arts*, 70 (1967), pp. 253–78

Segre, Cesare, and Françoise Fery-Hue, 'Bestiaires', in *Dictionnaire des lettres françaises, le Moyen Âge* (Paris, 1964), pp. 171–3

THE VALKYRIE

La Chanson des Nibelungen, trans. and ed. Danielle Buschinger and Jean-Marc Pastré (Paris, 2001)

Boyer, Régis, *La Religion des anciens scandinaves* (Paris, 1981)

Buschinger, Danielle, 'Les relations entre épopée française et épopée germanique: essai de position des problèmes', in *Au carrefour des routes d'Europe: La chanson de geste* (Aix-en-Provence, 1987), I, pp. 77–101

Dillmann, François-Xavier, *L'Edda: Récits de mythologie nordique par Snorri Sturluson* (Paris, 1991)

Dumézil, Georges, *Mythes et dieux de la Scandinavie ancienne* (Paris, 2000)

Krappe, A. H., 'The Walkyries', *Modern Language Review*, XXI (1926), pp. 55–73

Lacroix, Daniel W., 'Edda poétique', 'Saga' and 'Snorri Sturluson', in *Dictionnaire du Moyen Âge*, ed. Cl. Gauvard, A. de Libera and M. Zink (Paris, 2002), pp. 464–6, 1264–7, 1339–42

Müller, Ursula, and Ulrich Müller, ed., *Richard Wagner und sein Mittelalter* (Salzburg, 1989)

Simek, R., 'Walküren', *Lexicon des Mittelalters* (Munich, 1977–98), VIII, col. 1978

Steblin-Kamenskij, M. C., 'Valkyries and Heroes', *Arkiv für nordisk Filologi*, XCVII (1982), pp. 81–93

Tonnelat, Ernest, *La Légende des Nibelungen en Allemagne au XIXe siècle* (Paris, 1952).

This book had been finished when I received François Amy de la Bretèque's *L'Imaginaire médiéval dans le cinéma occidental* (Paris, 2004), which contains important details on the films cited here as well as other cinematographic works illustrating the medieval imaginary. This remarkable collection presents the Gothic imagination as seen through the cinema, including Roland, El Cid, Arthur, knights, Merlin, troubadours, Tristan and Iseult, Reynard and Robin Hood, and the Middle Ages of Walter Scott, Victor Hugo and Richard Wagner.

PHOTO ACKNOWLEDGEMENTS

AKG, Paris: pp. 60, 96, 118, 123, 130; Jean Bernard: p. 48; Bridgeman Images: pp. 22, 41, 159, 162 (Giaraudon), 197 (Babara Singer); BNF, Paris: pp. 27, 34, 139, 149, 173, 184; Collection Christophe L.: p. 136; Enguerrand: p. 79; Ikona: p. 178; Josse: p. 82; Oronoz: p. 77; Picture Desk: p. 98 (G.Dagli Orti); RMN: p. 88 (René-Gabriel Ojeda); Scala: pp. 85, 105 (Opera Metropolitana), 117; Shutterstock: p. 71 (Sergey Goryachev); TCD: pp. 31, 110, 160.